Agile Leadership and the Management of Change

Project Lessons from Winston Churchill and the Battle of Britain

By Mark Kozak-Holland

First Edition

Multi-Media Publications Inc.
Oshawa, Ontario

Agile Leadership and the Management of Change:
Project Lessons from Winston Churchill and the Battle of Britain

By Mark Kozak-Holland

Managing Editor:	Kevin Aguanno
Copy Editor:	Susan Andres
Typesetting:	Peggy LeTrent/Tak Keung Sin
Cover Design:	Tak Keung Sin

Published by:
Multi-Media Publications Inc.
Box 58043, Rosslynn RPO
Oshawa, ON, Canada, L1J 8L6

http://www.mmpubs.com/

Paperback	ISBN-13: 9781554890354
Adobe PDF ebook	ISBN-13: 9781554890361

Published in Canada. Printed simultaneously in Canada, the United States of America, and the United Kingdom.

CIP data available from the publisher.

Table of Contents

Dedication

To Jerry, my father, who instilled in me a determination to succeed.

I am incredibly indebted to my wife Sharon and my family (Nicholas, Jamie, and Evie) who have been so gracious in allowing me to continue with this writing project at the expense of our valuable time together.

Agile Leadership and the Management of Change

Acknowledgments

I would like to thank Kevin Aguanno for helping me to pull this book together and for providing his usual sound advice and guidance.

Agile Leadership and the Management of Change

Foreword

By David Whiting, stepson of Air Chief Marshal Hugh Dowding

Even though this book is primarily about project management and agility, I will comment on the important historical analogy that runs through the book. This analogy is remarkable because it demonstrates how a small team acting with agility, leadership, and purpose achieved a goal that was thought unachievable. Against all the odds, the British in September 1940 were able to inflict the first defeat on the German military forces that continued to be victorious right up to 1943.

In May 1940, as the British army was evacuated from Dunkirk, Winston Churchill, the new prime minister, faced a disaster and had to respond to an invasion threat. The problem was the United Kingdom economy was on a civilian footing, as household goods and new automobiles were still being built and diverting critical manufacturing resources and raw materials. Churchill had to respond with agility and put priority to the right areas. He had to bring together disparate organizations and set up a governance framework to support this.

When it came to the defense of the United Kingdom, the Air Council had prioritised Bomber over Fighter Command, and fighter production was still grounded in the antiquated practices of the First World War. One of Churchill's most important decisions was to prioritise fighter air defense and fighter production over everything. Churchill took the dramatic step of forming a new Ministry of Aircraft Production (MAP). He appointed a strong leader, Lord Beaverbrook (Max Aitken), someone he knew could turn fighter production around and whose leadership style would make an immediate impact at MAP.

In parallel, Churchill's decision to support Air Chief Marshal Hugh Dowding was significant. Dowding had created a structure for the new Royal Air Force (RAF) Fighter Command and needed Churchill's support in prioritizing resources for the United Kingdom's air defense.

Air Chief Marshal Hugh Dowding's Story

Dowding's story starts with his experience in the cold wet winter of 1914–15 (as he wrote, ankle deep in mud) as a flight commander with No. 9 (wireless) Squadron at Saint Omer, the Royal Flying Corps (RFC) Headquarters (the RFC's first wireless school) and his return to England in 1915 to set up another wireless experimental establishment at Brooklands. After some experiments there, "...a wireless transmitter was fitted into the Maurice-Farman; and Dowding claims to be the first person, certainly in England if not the world, to listen to a wireless telephone message from the air."[1] So Dowding well understood and could foresee the potential of Henry Tizard and his team's experiments with wireless echoes that would lead to the development of radar.

Dowding remained in the RAF after the war and eventually created RAF Fighter Command in 1936. The Air Council held to Trenchard's[2] old ideas of strategic bombing that the bomber will always get through. Therefore, the priority in the early days was on building bombers to send out to parts of the old British Empire. With the Air Council's support for Bomber command and the lack of fighter aircraft, Dowding had to come up with a different solution. Dowding had vision and was always fascinated by technology and its development. Thankfully, as the air marshal in charge of research and development, Dowding was in the right place at the right time to encourage and finance, through the Air Council of the RAF, the development of radar. Dowding pushed through the creation of the first Air Defence system using radar.

Dowding ensured that Fighter Command had the necessary tools, including his Operations Room at Bentley Priory, which integrated information from radar, raid plotting, and radio control of aircraft, Royal Observer Corp, and other sources into the system. In parallel, he worked out the complex and meticulous detail in the use of eight-gun fighters with which eventually to defeat the German attempt to gain air superiority over the United Kingdom.

Dowding was a determined and strong leader, features which sometimes brought him into conflict with his peers and superiors. His contemporaries, many of whom were jealous of his abilities, little understood him. Dowding foresaw that the air battle, when it came, would be to defend England from across the English Channel. He fought and eventually won the day to have fighter production increased to defend the homeland. He argued strongly that Fighter Command's role was to protect the United Kingdom and went against the then accepted wisdom of using the RAF's valuable resources to protect France, famously writing to the Air Ministry: "I believe that, if an adequate fighter force is kept in this country, if the fleet remains in being, and if Home Forces are suitably organized to resist invasion, we should be able to carry on the war single-handed for some time, if not indefinitely. But, if the Home Defence Force is drained away in desperate attempts to remedy the situation in France, defeat in France will involve the final, complete and irremediable defeat of this country."[3]

I believe that Dowding later considered that writing a letter he knew Churchill would see, combined with confronting Churchill at a meeting of the War Cabinet on 15 May 1940 with a graph of the predicted Hurricane losses if more were sent to France, were perhaps the most important decisions he made during the battle. He also put his career on the line. He had made a visit to France earlier and was astounded at the lack of a modern air defence system. The French system consisted of a man at the end of a telephone taking notes with a pencil and paper.

Lord Beaverbrook's Story

In contrast, Beaverbrook was an outsider who had a peer relationship with Churchill who respected his ability to get the job done, even though the two men argued vigorously. Beaverbrook would take a very different "no nonsense" business approach, and with remarkable speed, he was able to cut through red tape to accelerate production and to lock step the supply chain to the daily demands of RAF Fighter Command.

The Outcome

Dowding completed a sophisticated early warning system known as the "Dowding System." The tracking of wastage and the ability to direct Beaverbrook's Civilian Repair Operation were important parts of the recovery operation and the Fighter Supply Chain. In parallel, Beaverbrook managed to align his fighter supply chain closely to RAF Fighter Command demand, which involved his daily communication with Dowding. This was the first truly integrated air defence system, and with it, Dowding kept the battle over British territory, as pilots had a better chance of survival to regain the fight, and downed aircraft could be repaired or used for spare parts to keep others flying. His aircraft in France were blind without the benefit of swift guidance to the hostile target, thanks to his system.

During the Battle of Britain, Dowding's Fighter Command resisted the attacks of the Luftwaffe. Aside from the Fighter Command system, he marshalled resources behind the scenes and maintained a significant fighter reserve, while leaving his subordinate commanders' hands free to run the battle.

After the war, I think Beaverbrook told my mother that Dowding was third on Hitler's assassination list. Hitler realised that Dowding was the commander who was preventing him from gaining air supremacy of the British airspace to allow his planned land invasion. Beaverbrook's role was less obvious to the enemy at the time.

This integration of manufacturing to vectoring fighters to targets allowed Beaverbrook, Dowding, and Churchill to operate with agility and turn a disaster around unexpectedly with an unexpected victory. The logistics of these twin approaches are staggering; Dowding and Beaverbrook were responsible for both of them. It is impossible to comprehend the full genius of these extraordinary men without reading this fascinating and instructive book. In summary, Dowding and Beaverbrook were the architects to the Battle of Britain. There are very important lessons for today's business world in their leadership, approach, and execution of plan.

In the year that sees the publication of the first full-length biography since Basil Collier's *Leader of The Few* in 1957, it is gratifying, as the stepson of Hugh Dowding, to see at long last a well-deserved rejuvenation of his reputation. Mark Kozak-Holland is to be congratulated on a truly original work, which looks at an aspect of Dowding's genius not researched before and extracts lessons for today's business world.

David Whiting, December 2008.

Preface

As the world's economy becomes more integrated and organizations more interconnected, *agility* has become a more important factor than organizational size or economy of scale. An agile organization can better respond, in a timely way, to change and to external factors or events driving change. However, the road to organizational agility is not easy and requires a carefully planned transformation project based on the principles of agile leadership and management of change to drive it.

> "Agile . . . characterized by quickness of mind, resourcefulness, or adaptability in coping with new and varied situations . . . Applied to mental or intellectual matters, it suggests ready adaptability to change and adjust."
>
> —Webster's Third New International Dictionary

This book describes how an organization can be transformed to become more agile. However, this is not a new concept; it was exemplified in 1940 when Winston Churchill was in a similar situation.

The book follows Winston Churchill's progress as a prime minister (PM) and project manager (PM) managing his organization, the United Kingdom, in the summer of 1940. It examines how he planned and executed a transformation project to introduce organizational agility so that he could meet an immediate crisis, the most significant threat in five hundred years. It describes the strategies he took to overcome incredible odds. Not only did he have to stave off an imminent enemy invasion, but he also had to move the peacetime economy to one that could support a war. This meant acting with incredible agility, repairing the military supply chain, focusing slender resources on the immediate threat, unifying a disparate economy, and directing its output into immediate military use. With very little time, Churchill had to transform his organization through this project.

Obstructing his path, Churchill had to address institutionalized inertia and an establishment structure that resisted change. This meant he had to manage his audience in terms of aligning them to the change and setting expectations to the enormity of the task ahead. When operating within an uncertain and unpredictable environment, leaders have to be adaptive. An *agile* organization can allow the leader to turn a negative situation into a positive *opportunity*.

The Book's Organization

The book is organized into twenty-five chapters, following a timeline from May to October 1940 in the United Kingdom. It delves into all the aspects of Churchill's transformation project and uses the nine Knowledge Areas (KA)[1] advocated by the PMI Book of Knowledge (PMBoK) to increase our understanding of the project.

At the end of each chapter, key lessons and best practices are presented. Where appropriate, exercises have been added for educators to use in training and workshops.

The Reader

This book is for project managers (PMs) and business and information technology (IT) professionals who want to develop into more *agile* leaders and make their organizations and systems more agile. The path to organizational agility may not be easy because of the bureaucratic challenges of an organization. The goal is to provide the reader insights into steps that could be taken to lower the risk and increase the likelihood of success.

The Reader's Work Environment

In the past, when industry events such as product launches, marketing initiatives, or changes in legislation occurred, their impact was not apparent for weeks, months, or possibly years. Typically, in the past, such an event affected all organizations equally, so everyone had time to counter the event. However, emerging technologies and the Internet have altered the reaction time. Organizations have to understand these events in real time and react accordingly with countermeasures; otherwise, they could be quickly overwhelmed. For example, Shell had determined the 1973 Oil Crisis as a possibility using scenarios planning. Shell not only rode out the worst successfully but also moved from the eighth to the second largest oil company.

Organizational agility is becoming an inescapable feature to surviving in a rapidly changing business climate. It allows organizations to be competitive, meet the adaptive realities of today's world, and survive. Many organizations know the information to do this is there in the enterprise but are challenged in putting it in front of the right people, in the right timeframe to leverage it. This is partly because many institutional core systems were originally designed decades ago and are geared to a time horizon measured in years. As organizations adapt to changes in markets, finance, and other

17

variables, they seek to synchronize with other businesses at every level, and temporal integration becomes deeper, more comprehensive, and more important.[2] Time scales have gone from days to hours.

The Reader's Choice of the Book

There are several reasons why you might have chosen this book, for example:

- You are looking to transform your business to have the agility of a small organization to operate better in an uncertain and unpredictable environment and in a shorter time horizon.

- You are looking to understand better the transformation project, the effort required, and deliverables, so you can be a full participant.

- You want to mitigate the risk through strategies and avoid the pitfalls of the transformation.

- You want the transformation project to deliver a solution that meets the needs of the organization and that the organization widely accepts.

Problems Addressed by the Book

This book will help you start to solve the following in becoming agile:

- When to get started. An organization is facing a crisis, but the leaders cannot turn it around fast enough. The inability to make inroads comes down to the inability to trim down the scope, so it can be tackled as a transformation project.

- How to get started. Leaders fail to understand, clearly articulate, and prioritize the problems they face, so the vision and journey are not clear, and the transformation project becomes tactical and short term.

- Why get started. Institutional intransigence within the organization, an acceptance of the status quo, reluctance to take on the task in hand, and resistance to change. Leaders fail to put in place a communication plan and fail to put together the team to run the transformation project. The vision is not well communicated, the team fails to make an impact, and overall confidence wanes.

- What are the risks. Transformation projects are enterprise wide and complex by their nature. As a result, the risk is greater, and there is less organizational tolerance in missed deadlines. It requires a more holistic approach. Carefully assess the risks associated with the transformation project before committing to it.

- What if interest wanes. As important is keeping the organizational focus on the problems and the solution that the project will create. If interest wanes in the project, it is likely to be challenged or even abandoned.

- Where to get started. Leaders do not have adequate information (about the organization, market, competition).

- What technology options are available to the transformation project. What are the scope, costs, and risks associated with these?

- What to get started with. Every transformation project needs to address all aspects of the business, namely, process, people, and technology.

Background to the Book

Winston Churchill is widely regarded as one of the greatest leaders of the twentieth century. Although much has been written about Churchill, it must be stated that this is a business book about agility—foremost business and project management—and not just history (reliant on secondary research).

For me, the journey started while completing a services project in London, England. I was part of a team completing a business exploration engagement for a decision support solution. A welcomed visit to the cabinet war rooms (Storey's Gate) provided a pleasant surprise. As an IT professional, I was used to seeing decision-making environments and command-and-control systems. Wandering around the museum, it struck me that this was what I was looking at from today's perspective—something I had not expected to see in a 1940 time capsule.

My interest was peaked, and further research took me along the path to RAF Bentley Priory and Uxbridge (RAF Fighter Command and Group Headquarters). These both illuminated their strategic purpose and the level of integration for passing information with Storey's Gate. This was a complex integrated solution and for that, a transformation project was required.

On further examination, I discovered that what I was looking at was a project of massive complexity. This project delivered an early manifestation of today's systems—what we would refer to as command and control and decision support. In the twenty-first century, we refer to this as the Adaptive

Enterprise. It incorporated a number of modern inventions, such as radar and the electronic computer, as part of the solution

As I presented the story of Churchill's Adaptive Enterprise to various organizations, it became apparent that this project had been realized only because of Churchill's agility and his decisive abilities. It also became apparent that this period in time (May to October 1940) closely resembled the pace of today's rapidly changing business climate.

So how does this relate to the field of project management today? Many projects today are initiated with clear objectives, executive sponsorship, and healthy budgets, but they still fail. Other projects have impossible timescales and face intransigence and numerous obstacles in their way, and yet, they succeed. This is the story of one of the perceived successes.

As you go through this book, you will find many surprises, such as the fact that Churchill's transformation project encompassed everything we would face in a modern project today. Reading this book will help you manage your projects better. Consider whether you have ever faced a project with any of these features:

- Intolerable time constraints
- Intimidating scope
- Antiquated governance structure
- Organizational intransigence
- Competing groups vying for resources
- Continuously changing environment
- New obstacles appearing every day

- Available resources that have to be carefully distributed

If you have encountered any of these problems within a transformation project, then take heart. Churchill's project faced all these issues as he faced a battle for survival. The project operated under the most difficult circumstances and was still able to achieve something remarkable, and so can you.

If you have any ideas for improving this book, please contact me via e-mail. Your feedback can be incorporated into a future edition.

Mark Kozak-Holland
E-mail: mark.kozak-holl@sympatico.ca

CHAPTER ONE

Overview of the Book

Winston Churchill had a very lengthy career that spanned five decades. This *Lessons from History* book focuses on a relatively short period that starts in May 1940 and ends in October 1940. It relates to a perilous situation where the United Kingdom was on the brink of an invasion. This situation resulted in the Battle of Britain, which shifted the course of the Second World War.

The story is about the leadership of Churchill the PM, prime minister or better still project manager, who as he came into office in a period of calamitous change, faced a potential disaster. It was a major undertaking where someone had to step up and take control of the situation, a project that no one wanted—*a true project from hell*. It was a truly desperate situation for a nation that had been ignoring all the warning signs for the best part of a decade. In this tight time frame, it boiled down to finding and implementing a solution that would extend Churchill's limited forces and maximize their effectiveness.

> In today's world, we talk about agile leaders who are capable of assessing a complex situation and then modifying their strategies and resources to attain the best outcomes for their organization.

So what is so important about this period of history? Simply put, the outcome of it was truly colossal, and it still reverberates today. Had the Battle of Britain been lost, it would have taken the United Kingdom out of the war through a peace treaty or invasion. The Axis would have had complete mastery of Europe. We would be living in a different world today had it not been for the outcome of this one single project. A regime similar to the system, but less horrendous, survived under the Soviets in Eastern Europe up to 1989.

The significance of this story is reflected in a noteworthy 2003 poll run by the BBC[1] to vote for the "greatest Briton ever." Churchill won easily and beat out titans such as Darwin, Shakespeare, Newton, Nelson, and Brunel. He is widely regarded not only as one of the greatest British prime ministers but also one of the greatest leaders of the twentieth century, clearly, for what he achieved in this SPECIFIC period in his career. In addition, we will see how, against all odds, this project delivered a solution that not only met but also exceeded expectations; in fact, the outcome was very different from what everyone expected.

"Never in the field of human conflict was so much owed by so many to so few."[2] When Churchill spoke these words, it brought attention to RAF Fighter Command and specifically, the pilots. However, this was the tip of a very large organization that provided much broader functions.

As important as the Battle of Britain was, what truly differentiated Churchill were his long-term objectives for the war, which he planned and executed for from the first day he became PM. In today's world, we talk about agile leaders who are always looking forward and positioning for the continual and sustained success of the organization. They have the ability to see beyond the short term and not sacrifice the longer-term objectives for it. This requires a resilience and fortitude to stand up for what matters.

Churchill certainly possessed these qualities, as by September 1941 (three months prior to Pearl Harbor), the U.S. was supplying most of the United Kingdom's armaments through lend-lease. Furthermore, they were also supporting the Soviet Union (centre of the conflict), providing convoy escorts across the Atlantic, had replaced the British forces protecting Iceland, and President Roosevelt had pledged every effort to defeat Germany.

The book looks at the background—why the United Kingdom got itself into a desperate situation in May 1940 and was so grossly unprepared. It also looks at the scope of what Churchill had to do and delves into the intricacies of the situation facing him and the associated problems, and how under tremendous pressure, he had to turn this around. For example, not only did he have to stave off an imminent enemy invasion but also he had to move the peacetime economy to one that could support a war long term, and this required a massive change effort. The book looks at how Churchill did it—how a project was put together to deliver a solution that in turn transformed his organization into the modern-day equivalent of an Adaptive Enterprise so that it could adapt to this unexpected situation.

As we go through the story, the historical analysis is done through a modern lens, examining the project along with Churchill's actions and strategy. For example, communication management was critical, as Churchill had to boost morale and inspire his cabinet, government, and nation to continue a fight already considered lost. Churchill set up an intricate adoption plan using the sway of the media, which came under his influence.

Aimed at project managers and business professionals, the book extracts learnings from Churchill's experiences that can be applied to project management today. For example, through a governance framework, Churchill had to organize the institutions and resources around him deftly to maximum effect. He had to focus slender resources on the immediate threat, unify a disparate economy, and direct its output into immediate military use. All the time, he had to manage the situation and events happening around him.

The book examines the project from the PM's leadership style, his background, and the career that prepared him for the role of PM in the summer of 1940. From the disaster of Gallipoli (1915) to his time in the trenches (1916) to serving as the Minister of Munitions (1917), his experience acquainted him with similar problems he was to face in 1940. It also examines his personal work habits that made him so effective on a day-to-day basis and his overall influence on the people and organizations around him.

Beyond Churchill, the book examines his lieutenants (project leaders), specifically Beaverbrook, Dowding, and lesser so, Menzies, their roles in the project, and how their selection played a significant part in the story. As the project pans out, the book examines how the solution was created and implemented, using the emerging technologies of the day. Although these may be different to today's technologies, their application and outcome are similar, specifically in the use of information to enhance decision making. These parallels are relevant for modern business. The book looks at, in detail, the four components of the solution (intelligence gathering, supply chain, command and control, sense and respond) and the manner in which they were integrated into a cohesive solution that evolved over several iterations.

Finally, the book examines the actual events through the summer months and extrapolates the impact of the solution on the outcome. It looks at how the solution was put into operation, how it was measured, and what its overall impact was. The project had to get it right the first time and make the investments count.

Agile Leadership and the Management of Change

CHAPTER TWO

Background: Years Before September 1939

This chapter looks at the background to the project, the events that led to it, and how intransigence allowed problems to fester and get worse. It asks the question, at what point do you say enough is enough and start to take actions? It also starts to look at what differentiated Churchill from his colleagues and opponents.

Most people are very familiar with the rise of the Nazis who came into power in 1933 by taking advantage of a country in chaos and ruin, ravaged by a financial crisis, depression, and the Treaty of Versailles. In the United Kingdom and the West, there was little response as public support for another war was very limited. The Western economies were still recovering from the Depression. In fact, many senior British politicians thought that the Treaty had been too harsh on Germany, and leeway should be given. Over in the U.S., many believed that involvement in the First World War had been a mistake, and attempts were made to stay isolated.

Churchill did not share this view of the Nazis and recognized early what was happening. Although he was not in a position of power, he did what he could to call the Nazis ambitions out and grill the politicians in power who tried to ignore him and take no actions. By 1934, he was particularly concerned about the growth of the *Luftwaffe,* the German air force, which could strike directly at the United Kingdom.

In today's world, organizations need to pay close attention to events and changes in the business environment and prepare for worst-case situations. Techniques such as future scenario planning will better make potential options available to organizations, which then have the ability to react and respond through a project should a series of events turn for the worst. In 1973, Shell did this very effectively in reacting to the oil crisis.

Churchill's peers and the press considered him a maverick, a loose cannon, out of touch with the realities of the time, and a dangerous eccentric who could trigger a war. Even though in 1929, he had held the second highest position in government as the Chancellor of the Exchequer. Somewhat at odds with public opinion, his career was over, and he was out in the wilderness.

On the other hand, he became a magnet for a small group of worried people. These included anxious intelligence officers who brought him statistics on air production in Germany, showing rearmament and contravention of the Treaty of Versailles. Churchill was unafraid of using this information in heavily criticizing the new Prime Minister Baldwin, as he spoke to the House on the slow pace of air defence research. By 1935, Churchill was perceived as a conduit for getting issues on the table and someone who never wavered from his view.

By 1936, the situation worsened with the Nazis occupation of the Rhineland demilitarized zone. In the same year, the Nazi propaganda machine used the Olympic Games, held in Germany, to promote an image of a peaceful and tolerant Germany.

By 1937, Churchill had become a voice and rallying point as he wrote over one hundred columns mostly warning of the Nazi intentions and Europe's impending doom. The new Prime Minister Neville Chamberlain was more proactive in looking for a solution, but with First World War guilt, he was an ambassador for peace and tried to mollify Hitler whom he thought he could manage through a policy of appeasement. The mood in popular opinion pushed him to seek out a policy in which British interest could be accomplished without entanglement in war, as he believed the British public had no appetite for another world war.

By 1938, Chamberlain's misguided negotiations had played Czechoslovakia into Hitler's hands. He was a businessman, and he thought he could handle Hitler. Worse still, it led to a Nazi-Soviet non-aggression pact as Stalin, who had been looking for a political and military agreement with Britain and France, became nervous as he saw the Nazi Germany border get closer to the Soviet Union. Churchill, the maverick, repeatedly attacked Chamberlain and the government on their inability to halt the slide to war, urging them to stand up to Hitler. Churchill was seen as someone with moral conviction who could pick up a cause and stay true to it, and his stature grew.

Figure 2.1. Chamberlain with Hitler in Munich 1938. (Source: http://www.signalalpha.com/html/world_war_two.html.)

In today's world, changing events initiate projects. However, the response needs to be very rapid, and so the project, vision, and scope need to be thought through, already in place, and well understood in relation to the planned response scenarios. This also requires a project team in position to enact the project according to available options.

Conclusion

The road to the Second World War very much came down to the inability of Western politicians to say no. Churchill, a historian, understood early on what was happening, and he was astute enough to maximize the impact of valuable information he had collected and build up his case. He recognized that one of the chief goals of a project manager (or any leader for that matter) is to rally people to a cause and to do this requires considerable credibility gained through self-belief, steadfastness, courage, and integrity to the cause. By 1940, through his actions, he had become a real alternative to the status quo.

Key Lessons

In today's projects:

- Agile leaders make information widely available to encourage discussion and debate.

- Agile leaders stay connected, are open, and encourage networks to form.

- Agile leaders know the failure to adapt to change is rooted in the organization's past history of success, conventional wisdom, and memories. In other words, the organization culture can inhibit change or the need for it.

- Agile leaders are well informed; they read, study, and seek challenging assignments.

And:

- Communication Management (PMBoK KA)— Where possible, stay true to a direction in which you believe. This will build confidence and rally people/groups towards it. Often, the organization may be in denial.

- Risk Management (PMBoK KA)—

  o Carefully assess the risks associated with an initiative or project before committing to it.

  o Review any quantitative evidence available related to the issues and risks.

  o In accepting a transformation project, make sure you have the ability and authority to enable changes to reach project objectives.

Educators

In today's projects:

- Discuss Churchill's approach to rallying support for an initiative. In light of this, how feasible is the role of a maverick in today's organization?

CHAPTER THREE

Changing Face of War September 1939–May 1940

This chapter looks at how technology had changed war, so when it broke out, the Allies were grappling in how to respond, grounded in the mindset of the First World War. This is important for today's PMs in how to keep abreast of new technologies and their impact.

In 1939 on the eve of the Second World War, Churchill had gained enough credibility that the public demanded to bring him back. Chamberlain believed that Churchill's inclusion in the cabinet would frustrate his efforts to appease Hitler. After the invasion of Poland, Chamberlain declared war and reluctantly brought Churchill into a war cabinet as First Lord of the Admiralty. Although unwanted by his cabinet colleagues, they needed him to maintain credibility with the changing public mood. The public began to see him not as a warmonger but someone who could rouse the nation to fight—a backbone of the government.

> Today, many organizations struggle to bring forward people for the top project jobs. Ask the PMs in the organization whom they would support, and natural leaders—those with credibility and weight to make a real difference with projects—will be propelled forward.

The surprise attack on Poland should have been a wake-up call for the Allies. There was no declaration of war, and the attack came when the defenders least expected it—in the early hours of Sunday morning. The Blitzkrieg started with Luftwaffe air strikes at airfields, destroying aircraft still on the ground. By winning air superiority without a major air battle, the Luftwaffe could then concentrate attacks on ground defences coordinated closely to rapidly mobile mechanized divisions. Agility, mobility, and highly advanced communications were needed. Two weeks into the campaign, the Soviet Union marched into Eastern Poland under the Nazi-Soviet non-aggression pact, highlighting the follies of Chamberlain's appeasement policy (chapter 2). Fighting on two fronts, the defeat came to Poland quickly, and this was used as propaganda to enhance the profile of the Wehrmacht, the German armed forces, as Hitler was trying to intimidate countries into submission without a fight. Chamberlain's half-hearted declaration of war missed the opportunity for a counter strike on the thinly defended Western border to give hope to the Polish ally.

Figure 3.1: Attack on Poland. (Courtesy of Illustrated London News.)

In today's world, organizational leaders need to be prepared for worst-case scenarios with a plan that is ready to launch into a project quickly and that responds to a scenario.

The next nine months was then followed by a *phony war* as the United Kingdom and France dug in and waited in the trenches and behind the Maginot line. Both countries expected a prolonged static war like experienced in the First World War, and the British Army had gone out with the same strategy and tactics. It was equipped to wage colonial warfare and to police a global commercial empire.

Through the 1930s, new emerging technologies had spurred the rapid development of military planes, tanks, and motorized vehicles. Even though the Western powers had these in greater numbers, they were deployed and used to support a static war. Elementary equipment, such as wireless sets, was lacking, as mobility was not seen as critical as supporting infantry was. The Allies had failed to realize how technology had changed war.

> **Today's leaders need to understand how competitors are reacting to change. Are they able to take advantage of a situation? What is giving them an edge—is it an emerging technology? How is it being deployed? The important lesson is to be proactive and not sit back.**

Churchill, as First Lord of the Admiralty, was prepared to sponsor new emerging technologies. He accelerated the research and experimentation of Asdic radar, used in the detection of submarines, and introduced it into ships of the fleet. He understood the tactical and strategic advantages it would provide.

Churchill was proactive and tried to push the neutral countries (Norway, Holland, Sweden, Denmark, Switzerland, and Belgium) together to create a united front against Nazism:

> "Each one hopes that if he feeds the crocodile enough, that the crocodile will eat him last."[1]

Churchill also wanted to take the war forward proactively through the pre-emptive occupation of the neutral Norwegian iron-ore port of Narvik and the iron mines in Kiruna, Sweden, in February 1940. However, Chamberlain and the War Cabinet disagreed, so the operation was delayed. This gave the Germans the initiative, and in April 1940, they invaded Denmark and Norway through a simultaneous operation. As paratroopers were dropped from the air to capture strategic positions, troops emerged from merchant ships to seize key harbours, and seaborne landings were made. The Air Force quickly established control of the skies and supported the army and the Kriegsmarine, German Navy, a fraction of the size of the Allied Navy. Mobile troops quickly traversed roads thought impassable. The whole invasion happened so quickly it caught the Allies out, despite British efforts. It was a foretaste of what was to come. Churchill coordinated an Allied response, but it was unsynchronized and too slow.

> In today's projects, the new mantra has become agility, and PMs need to be proactive in understanding changes in technology, managing expectations, and mitigating risks.

Conclusion

The early events of the Second World War highlighted how technology had changed war and how the Allies were unable to grapple with it. As Churchill acquired power, he was able to recognize that one of the chief goals of a project manager is to understand changes and be proactive and agile. Therefore, by May 1940, he had established much credibility and had become a real hope for the public.

Key Lessons

In today's projects:

- Agile leaders are proactive in managing expectations and mitigating risks.

- Agile leaders stay abreast of changes in emerging technology.

- Agile leaders understand how competitors are reacting to change, so they can take advantage of a situation.

- Agile leaders know that the transformation project is a dynamic voyage full of challenges.

- Agile leaders weigh the consequences of inaction to determine if it is worse than action.

And:

- Scope Management (PMBoK KA)—

  o Be prepared for worst-case scenarios with a plan that is ready to launch into a project quickly and that responds to a particular scenario.

Educators

- In the context of today's business environment, discuss the difference in Churchill's and Chamberlain's views of the situation. Would this be common in today's world?

CHAPTER FOUR

Churchill Becomes PM

This chapter looks at how Churchill acquired the project and took immediate actions.

The United Kingdom in May 1940 faced a desperate situation as Chamberlain had stalled for peace, hoping he could manage his way out without declaring war. The United Kingdom was hopelessly unprepared for a modern war (chapter 3). On May 8, the British Parliament questioned his handling of the Norwegian campaign with the loss of about 4,000 British troops and the occupation of the country. In a vote of confidence, his majority crashed as politicians lost faith in his failed leadership. A "coalition" government was desperately needed, but the opposition parties, senior Labour figures, opposed forming this under Chamberlain. They firmly believed that the only leader credible enough to take over was Churchill, and they made this a condition.

On May 10, Axis forces invaded the West (Holland, Belgium, and Luxembourg) by air and land (see figure 4.1). Agile Axis forces quickly overran Eben Emale, the linchpin of Belgium's entire defence and a fortress thought impenetrable, in a few hours with little loss of life. Luxembourg was occupied within a day, and the situation in Holland deteriorated. Reaction times had become enormously compressed, and the Allies failed to grasp changes in modern warfare driven by agility and communications (chapter 3).

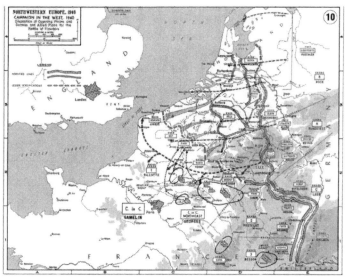

Figure 4.1. The 1940 campaign in France and the Low Countries. (Courtesy of U.S. Department of Defense.)

In Parliament, the pressure for change was enormous, and Chamberlain was forced to resign. His right hand man Lord Halifax was offered the project leadership, but he turned it down. As a second choice, Churchill was reluctantly offered it. Within Churchill's own party, many thought Churchill was a major risk, holding him responsible for the major military disaster at Gallipoli (1915). Offering Churchill the leadership was a desperate act, yet no one was prepared to stick his neck out for this project because the United Kingdom was facing a worsening situation and insurmountable problems. Even through there were no takers to lead the project, it did not matter to Churchill, as he saw this as part of his destiny and a privilege to be in the position.

> **In today's world, this may all seem incredulous, but even though Churchill had been marginalized politically, he had built up backbench credibility across the parties. He was fully respected by the opposition who gladly accepted him as the leader of a unified team. All along, he had consistently predicted the outcome of Chamberlain's policies correctly, and he never faltered or strayed from this core message (chapter 3).**

Why would anyone today even consider a risky project such as this? Why did Churchill take on the project? In short, he was ready for it, mentally prepared, as for a decade he had clearly seen the slide towards war and the government mistakes (chapter 2). Because of his position and previous experience, he had a better view of the Axis military than most people did. He was able to ascertain what was required to get through the short term and how. He was also cognizant of the consequences of the defeat of the United Kingdom.

> **In today's projects, accepting the responsibility for a project requires understanding scope, basic problems, organizational desire to solve, and the related risks. As a PM, you may not have a say or a choice in leading a project that is put upon you. Therefore, in such a compromised situation, it is important to set expectations as to what can be done and highlight concerns and risks. In addition, going through a scenario planning exercise with the project team upfront is important to prepare for different possible outcomes. Churchill envisaged several outcomes, as he had time to plan his approach before he accepted the project.**

Churchill was the only senior government cabinet member not ready to admit defeat. He knew he had a split in his party with the majority of senior members leaning towards peace because of their concerns over preserving the status quo. He repeatedly invited former Prime Minister Lloyd George into the War Cabinet, even though a bitter open feud existed with Chamberlain on his outspoken views. Keeping the British Empire in tact was more in important than the fate of the United Kingdom and Europe. Yet Churchill followed the logic of "better in than out" and kept his adversaries in the cabinet to the annoyance of his supporters. A shrewd move or a noble gesture—he wanted a united front for the public.

> **In today's projects, creating the right mix of people for the project team is a prerequisite for success, specifically, bringing people from across organizational boundaries to help with adoption and buy-in to the project.**

On May 13, Churchill faced Parliament for the first time as leader and wanted to show he was serious. He delivered one of the most memorable speeches ever as he dedicated himself and the nation to the project. No one had addressed the British in this manner:

> ...I have nothing to offer but blood, toil,
> tears, and sweat. We have before us an ordeal
> of the most grievous kind. We have before us
> many, many months of struggle and suffering.
> You ask, what is our policy? I say it is to
> wage war by land, sea, and air. War with all
> our might and with all the strength God has
> given us, and to wage war against a monstrous
> tyranny never surpassed in the dark and
> lamentable catalogue of human crime. That
> is our policy. You ask, what is our aim? I can

answer in one word. It is victory. Victory at all costs....[1]

In today's world, when taking over a project, a well thought out communications strategy is essential for setting the right tone for the overall project objectives. The more problematic a situation, the more important the kick-off meeting is to instill confidence into the project team and stakeholders.

Conclusion

As Churchill took over, he took steps to boost the confidence of British politicians who recognized the depth of his commitment to the project. He wanted to show he was serious, and he did when the internment of Germans began in the United Kingdom on May 12. Churchill's ascent to PM was not a given. Following a shaky start, it was unprecedented in that it would eventually extend over a lengthy period of six years.

Key Lessons

In today's projects:

- Agile leaders are ready to take over a new project and can create a plan quickly.

- Agile leaders display honesty, sincerity, integrity, and candour in all their actions.

- Agile leaders embrace uncertainty, ambiguity, and impermanence.

- Agile leaders are courageous and have the perseverance to reach an objective, even with seemingly insurmountable obstacles.

  And:

- Scope Management (PMBoK KA)—

    o Once the objectives of a project are clear, focus on the scope, what is in and out. Determine the organizational desire to solve the problems, the level of commitment and resources.

- Communication Management (PMBoK KA)—

    o Have a communication plan ready as early as possible to boost stakeholder confidence.

- Human Resource Management (PMBoK KA)—

    o Evaluate the as-is staff for a project team; do not rush to remove; look at how they can be evolved into a to-be team. In a fractured project, unity of the project team could be a priority.

Educators

- Discuss, in the context of today's projects, the importance of the PM setting the right tone for a project at the outset.

CHAPTER FIVE

Churchill Assesses the Problems

This chapter looks at how the situation deteriorated in less than a week into a near catastrophe. Churchill had to assess and prioritize the problems around him quickly.

In today's world, many project managers have little choice in saying "no" to an opportunity that is thrust upon them, especially one that is already in flight. They have to make the most of it and quickly get a grip.

By May 13, the military situation in Western Europe had declined rapidly. In the Battle of Flanders, Dutch troops withdrew to their final defence line. In France, the astounding speed of the invasion created a level of panic in the Allied forces as two armoured columns tore a fifty-mile gap into the defences. The front line and supply systems were static and not designed for mobile war (chapter 3).

> **Any project manager walking into a volatile situation needs first to assess the overall situation quickly to better understand the landscape, pain points, politics, and what needs to be addressed first. Actions may be required immediately in a fast-changing situation. This is what Churchill had to do.**

On May 14, the French Premier Paul Reynaud put pressure on Churchill to help with the defence of France by sending more fighter squadrons. The fighter loss rates were unsustainable. Although Churchill was aware of the problems facing the United Kingdom, in coming into power he had a significant disadvantage as a new PM. His short tenure in the position meant he was not well informed in French politics and the authenticity of these demands.

> **A new project manager very often will be under pressure to address certain issues and drive the project in a particular way to meet specific agendas—thus the importance of reading the landscape correctly and making the right assessments.**

On the morning of May 15, French Prime Minister Paul Reynaud telephoned Churchill and said, "We have been defeated. We are beaten; we have lost the battle."[1] Churchill reminded Reynaud of the First World War and the times the Allied lines had been breached only to be plugged later. However, by the end of the same day, Holland surrendered to a force whose innovative combination of aircraft, fast armour, infantry, and modern communications demonstrated an understanding of the revolution in military tactics (chapter 4). Worse still for Churchill, the Royal Air Force (RAF) had lost nearly 250 aircraft or 25% of its strength.

Figure 5.1. Hurricanes in France were overwhelmed. (Courtesy of Crown copyright.)

On May 16, Churchill, wasting no time, proactively flew to Paris to meet with Reynaud, to assess the situation personally, and to "talk up" resistance. When he got there, he saw the gravity of the situation as the French government was burning archives and preparing to evacuate the capital. Churchill asked General Gamelin, "Where is the strategic reserve?" which had saved Paris in the First World War. "There is none," Gamelin replied. Churchill later described this as the "single most shocking moment in his life."[2]

A new project manager needs to get into the front line of the organization, out among the troops, to understand the situation clearly and to dig deep to ratify the problems and their priority for resolution.

On the same day, the Air Chief Marshal of RAF Fighter Command, Hugh Dowding, wrote a letter that challenged Churchill over sending more fighter squadrons to France. Dowding recognized when to cut losses for the defence of the United Kingdom. Churchill took this letter very seriously, and this created a dilemma for him because he had personally promised these to Reynaud. In the end, squadrons were sent but operated in France during the day and then returned at night to England. This action further strained the Allied relationship.

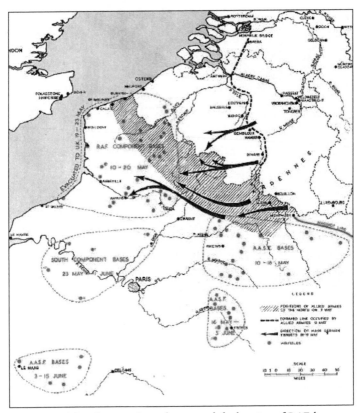

Figure 5.2. Map showing Axis advance and the location of RAF bases. (Courtesy of Crown copyright.)

In addition to air defence, Churchill was acutely aware of the following major problems faced by the United Kingdom:

- Lack of confidence in government circles around him

- The public unawareness of the seriousness of the current situation in France

- The economy not on war footing

- Lack of clear priorities as to where to focus the fight, as there was no single minister in charge of prosecuting the war

- The public unprepared for a total war and all the sacrifices that went with it

> **A new project manager has to stand his ground, keep his composure, and lay out the problems in priority. He needs to negotiate agreements on these problems so a strategy can be developed with requirements carefully understood and scoped out.**

The scale of the Axis advance was becoming apparent by May 17, as Allied forces were becoming separated by rapidly advancing armoured columns towards the Channel coast that was only seventy miles away. The armoured columns outrunning their supply lines were able to refuel at French gas stations not destroyed in time. Churchill clearly understood the Axis plan was to outflank the Allied forces in Belgium. He feared that the British Expeditionary Force (BEF) would be cut off if the French forces on the Western flank did not rally.

Conclusion

Within days of taking over the project, Churchill was thrown deep into the cauldron of war. Within the first week, the situation was disastrous, but Churchill kept his composure and his resolve, remained resolute to cause, stuck to a plan, and continued to look for a resolution to the most pressing problems.

Key Lessons

In today's projects:

- Agile leaders constantly assess the situation and monitor brewing issues so if things deteriorate, they can respond rapidly.

- Agile leaders are fair-minded and show fair treatment to everyone (Churchill's reaction to Dowding's letter).

  And:

- Risk Management (PMBoK KA)—

  o Focus on analyzing the risk first with the most pressing problems as defined by the core team.

- Planning Process (PMBoK)—

  o Develop a plan quickly and stick to it when the going gets tough and chaotic.

- Communication Strategy—

  o Be prepared to roll out a communication plan quickly to support the main plan and the management of change process.

Educators

- Discuss Dowding's challenge to Churchill—was it warranted; did he take a personal risk?

- Churchill was a leader under pressure, yet he stuck to plan. Discuss this in the context of today's business environment.

CHAPTER SIX

Last Gasp Effort

This chapter looks at how the project deteriorated. Churchill had to manage the desperate situation and make a monumental decision whether to stand and fight or evacuate.

On May 17, the Axis armoured columns halted, fearful of a counter strike to the wings, and this allowed the infantry and supply lines to draw near. Worried about different scenarios, Churchill asked for plans to be readied, under the codenamed Operation Dynamo, for the possible evacuation through Dunkirk of the British Expeditionary Force (BEF). He considered this a remote possibility and a precautionary move. He also, with some foresight, asked his chiefs of staff to prepare a paper on the prospects of the United Kingdom carrying the war alone.

> In today's world, PMs need to be well prepared for critical situations with worst-case scenarios in their plans, so they are able to execute contingencies quickly when needed (chapter 3).

By May 18, Churchill was having serious doubts about the Allies' ability to win the battle in Belgium and northern France. The Allied armies had still failed to take advantage of the enemy halt and continued to pull away towards the coast, fearing encirclement.

Figure 6.1. Map of Axis advance and the trapped armies in the North. (Source: http://www.brandonatwar.co.uk/dunkirk.jpg.)

On May 19, an all-important meeting between Churchill and the War Cabinet determined only two options for the BEF. The first was to move back to the channel ports, but this could shatter the fragile relationship with the French. The second was to move west to rejoin the Allied Southern armies, but this would lose the channel ports (Boulogne, Calais, and Dunkirk) and further undermine the Belgian army. They decided on the former and communicated this to the British commander in the field, Lord Gort.

> In today's world, a PM needs to keep a high-level view
> of the project, understand the impact of decisions and
> actions, and carefully consider the loyalties of stakeholders.
> Churchill demonstrated loyalties to his ally, even though
> the relationship was getting strained and confidence was
> decreasing by the day.

Churchill knew he had serious public relations
problems in the United Kingdom with the British public
(his primary stakeholders) who were completely unaware of
the grave situation in France. That evening, in his first radio
broadcast to the nation, he reset expectations on the possibility
of defeat: "Our task is not only to win the battle—*but to win
the war.* After this battle in France abates its force, there will
come the battle for our Island—for all that Britain is, and all
that Britain means. That will be the struggle. In that supreme
emergency we shall not hesitate to take every step, even the
most drastic, to call forth from our people the last ounce and
the last inch of effort of which they are capable. The interests of
property, the hours of labour, are nothing compared with the
struggle of life and honour, for right and freedom, to which we
have vowed ourselves."

Churchill was preparing the public for the next battle
and wanted it to be seen as a battle of good against evil. This
was to stiffen resolve and dispense ideas about suing for peace:

> "...behind the Armies and Fleets of Britain
> and France—gather a group of shattered
> States and bludgeoned races: the Czechs, the
> Poles, the Norwegians, the Danes, the Dutch,
> the Belgians—upon all of whom the long
> night of barbarism will descend, unbroken
> even by a star of hope, unless we conquer, as
> conquer we must; as conquer we shall."[1]

Figure 6.2. Churchill's radio broadcast. (Source: FDR-Library, Photos of WW2 Collection.)

The PM in today's changing world needs to monitor constantly where the project team and stakeholders are relative to their expectations of the project by asking questions, probing, and then updating the communications plan and constantly communicating.

On May 20, French Prime Minister Reynaud replaced his commander-in-chief. Weygand immediately concocted new tactics to contain the invasion. However, on the same day, the Axis armoured columns restarted their advance and reached the English Channel that evening with forward units, cutting the Northern Allied armies off. Churchill kept his poise on this disastrous day.

On May 21, Churchill, depressed at the lack of information and unfolding events, flew back to France. He met with Weygand who convinced him of a combined attack from the North and South on the Axis armoured columns.

Gort launched a hastily prepared attack on the same day with heavily armoured British tanks at the Battle of Arras. While initial gains were very good, low infantry numbers and the lack of planning meant these gains were lost as Axis forces quickly built up. This action sent fear into the Axis high command that their armoured divisions were overstretched. As a result, these columns were slowed down and, with that, the BEF was inevitably encircled. Regrettably, lack of time in planning and lining up of resources meant the attack could not be sustained.

> **The PM in today's world needs to be on the pulse of the project and react with agility. Churchill understood the desperation of the situation and the need for a concerted strike back.**

Gort continued to pull out of the encirclement between May 22 and 23. The Battle of Arras had been a last throw of the dice. On May 24, the Axis armoured divisions halted fifteen miles from Dunkirk, a very controversial decision as Göring predicted his Luftwaffe could prevent an evacuation and finish off the BEF. Under the operational doctrine, attacking cities was not part of the normal task for armoured units because of the disadvantage of fighting in close quarters.

Conclusion

In the first two weeks after Churchill became PM, he had managed an ever desperate and deteriorating situation. He took the monumental decision to stand and fight, rather than evacuate so as not to further strain the Allied relationship. However, the speed of the demise of the Allied forces was astonishing, as in two weeks, the Allies had lost more territory than in four years in the First World War. Churchill was now going to be fighting for the survival of the project. Fortunately, he had some contingency plans laid down.

Key Lessons

In today's projects:

- Agile leaders evaluate response options and plan contingencies in line with developing issues.

- Agile leaders need to remind the organization that the penalty of inaction can be much worse than the action itself.

And:

- Scope Management (PMBoK KA)—

  o Have contingency plans that have been thought through in place for worst-case scenarios.

- Communication Management (PMBoK KA)—

  o Continuously collect information on the project to be on the pulse.

Educators

- Discuss at what point in a project it becomes beneficial to lay contingency plans down. What factors would stimulate this?

CHAPTER SEVEN

Dunkirk and the End of the Battle of France

This chapter looks at how Churchill, faced with the destruction of the BEF, is left with no option but to evacuate, straining the Allied relationship to the breaking point.

On May 24, with Boulogne captured, the Allied Northern armies were retreating to the channel ports of Calais and Dunkirk. Based on Enigma decodes, Churchill knew that the Axis army commanders wanted to encircle and destroy these armies. Belgium was ready to give up, as too much territory had been lost.

> In today's world, a PM needs to keep a macro view of the project at all times.

Churchill's hesitation in the evacuation of the BEF was down to its potential impact on the military campaign in the West swaying the equilibrium towards the Axis forces and a shattering effect on the already dithering relationship with his Allies. It would also be a logistical nightmare, with few ships available, not enough time to complete such a large evacuation, and the requirement of a large number of civilian watercraft. With unprotected beaches, the potential for huge losses of troops would require a large presence of military ships and fighters to provide cover and protection. Churchill knew it would be unlikely that he could land another army on the continent for at least five years. He also knew that the United Kingdom required ground forces to fend off an invasion as the Navy and Air Force might not be enough.

On May 25, French Premier Reynaud sent Churchill an angry cable criticizing the British withdrawal from Arras. This infuriated Churchill because he had been misled about Amiens, which the French army had failed to take. It was evident that Weygand's plan (chapter 6) for combined north and south attacks had failed. Even worse, the French now proposed to explore the possibilities of a friendly settlement with an approach to the Italian Dictator Mussolini. France would give up German-speaking territories, and the United Kingdom would make small colonial concessions. The Anglo-French Alliance was starting to crack.

On May 26, Churchill and Halifax, his number 2 person, openly disagreed about the approach to Mussolini in the first daily War Cabinet meeting. The situation was desperate for Churchill, but he preferred nothing be done until the fate of the BEF was known. He also referenced previous failed peace deals (chapter 2) and the likely demoralizing effect on the public with such a move.

> **In today's world, losing project stakeholder support is bad enough but loss of the core-project team support usually means the PM will be fighting for the survival of the project.**

On the same day, Calais was lost. Both Churchill with the War Cabinet and the commander of the army Field Marshal Gort decided independently that the only course of action left was to pull the BEF out. The evacuation of the Northern Allied armies (500,000 British, French, and Belgian) from the northern pocket in Belgium and Pas-de-Calais began with the launch of Operations Dynamo and Ariel. This complex operation required hundreds of vessels. Getting any troops out was going to be difficult with initial predictions for 45,000 men. Soldiers fit to fight left first, the injured, last. Churchill's foresight and contingency plans helped kick in the evacuation.

Figure 7.1: The Chaos on Dunkirk Beach. (Source: http://history.howstuffworks.com/world-war-ii/nazi-germany-conquers-france5.htm.)

Likewise, in today's world, the PM needs to recognize a losing situation—when to cut losses and resort to contingency plans.

On May 27, Churchill presented to the War Cabinet the paper prepared by the chiefs of staff on the prospects of the United Kingdom carrying the war alone. It stated, "It is impossible to say whether or not the U.K. could hold out in all circumstances. The enemy's opening attack would likely be an air attack. The crux of the whole problem is the air defence of the country…should the enemy succeed in establishing a force with its vehicles, our army forces have not got the offensive power to drive it out."[1]

> In today's world, the PM needs to maintain a macro view. Churchill kept the macro view, even with the complexity of the evacuation, and a focus on likely future events for which the Air Force was critical

On May 28, Belgium surrendered after a deliberate delay by King Leopold III to help Operation Dynamo. At the War Cabinet meeting, the Italian proposal was brought up again, resulting in a stalemate between Churchill and Halifax. However, when Churchill addressed the full cabinet (of twenty-five members) with the words "whatever happens at Dunkirk, we will fight on,"[2] he received an outburst of emotional support for his position, which resulted in Halifax's backing down. It was the right decision, as Mussolini intended to declare war on England and France on June 5.

> In today's world, the PM should be prepared to battle it out for the support of the core project team and for the survival of the project itself. Churchill's judgment turned out to be correct. He was uninformed of the wider support he had

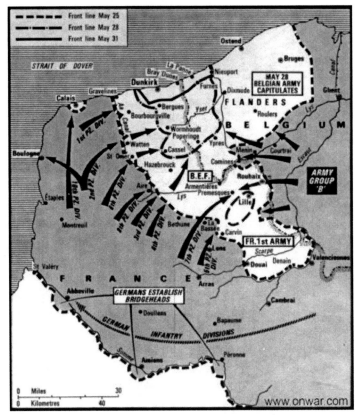

Figure 7.2. Map of the front line May 25–31. (Source: http://www.onwar.com/maps/wwii/blitz/dunkirk40.htm.)

On May 29, 47,300 British and French troops were evacuated, steadily increasing to 53,823 on the 30th, peaking at 68,000 on the 31st, and 64,429 on June 1st. At this point, it became a night operation because of the high warship losses. On June 2, another 26,200 were evacuated, so all the BEF was now out, and on the last night of June 3, 26,700 French troops were evacuated, bringing the total to 224,686 British and 121,445 French and Belgian (plus German prisoners of war). In all, 338,226 troops were evacuated by 900 vessels (naval, commercial, and private). Most French troops were relanded in France to continue the fight.

Figure 7.3: The disaster of Dunkirk where the BEF lost 90% of its heavy equipment. (Source: http://history.howstuffworks.com/world-war-ii/nazi-germany-conquers-france5.htm.)

Clearly, Dunkirk was a complete disaster as the BEF lost 90% of its heavy equipment. The Allies got away with little but the shirts on their backs. A staggering 75,000 vehicles and trucks and 400 tanks, along with 650,000 tons of arms, ammunition, and supplies were left behind (1,200 field guns, 1,350 anti-aircraft and anti-tank guns, 11,000 machine guns), all of which were sorely needed to defend the United Kingdom.

Around 200 ships and 177 aircraft were lost, of which 109 were precious fighters. The Axis lost 240 aircraft.

Conclusion

The initial intent was to recover around 45,000 troops, therefore, so many troops getting out was a miracle. Even though the army had been saved, Dunkirk was a disaster in terms of losses of fighters, naval ships, and military equipment. It also put Churchill's position as PM at considerable risk.

Key Lessons

In today's projects:

- Agile leaders move quickly, responding to presented opportunities with a thought out plan.

- Agile leaders enact response options based on preplanned contingencies in line with the issues.

  And:

- Scope Management (PMBoK KA)—

  o Keep a macro view of the project/objectives, and remind others of it when things get off track.

- Communication Management (PMBoK KA)—

  o Check continuously for support towards the project from within the project core team.

Educators

- Discuss the impact of Churchill's foresight and contingency plans in the evacuation of Dunkirk.

At what point, do you cut your losses in today's projects?

- Discuss steps you could take to maintain a macro view in today's projects.

CHAPTER EIGHT

Aftermath of Dunkirk

This chapter looks at how Churchill's position as PM was at considerable risk and how he turned things around with the most significant speech of his career.

On June 4, the Dunkirk evacuation ended. Although the British had evacuated a greater number of exhausted troops, most of its heavy fighting equipment, enough for ten divisions and over two hundred ships, was lost (chapter 8). Dunkirk was a complete disaster in terms of equipment loss. In retrospect, the BEF faced complete elimination, and for Churchill, there was no other choice but to evacuate.

Figure 8.1. Defeat at Dunkirk. (Courtesy of Crown copyright.)

> **In today's world, project timing is everything in terms of communication and delivery. As the project twists and turns, a PM needs to be in tune with the pulse of the project and know when to communicate and deliver key morale raising talks/speeches, especially with stakeholders.**

On the evening of June 4, Churchill knew he had a split in the War Cabinet (Halifax and Chamberlain) and discontent with senior members in Parliament. He was in a shaky position, and a further loss in support meant he could be quickly evicted from power. However, when he addressed the junior members of his government in a private meeting, he was bolstered by their emotional support, as they rallied to him and the cause. Through the evacuation, Churchill kept repeating, "Whatever happens at Dunkirk, the British will fight on,"[1] a resoluteness to cause.

Churchill went to address Parliament, and he knew that not in nine hundred years had Britain faced such a humiliating defeat. He had to make the most of it and spin it into a victory of morale. Churchill explained the sequence of events and that initial expectations for evacuating 45,000 troops were vastly superseded by the evacuation of 338,226. This was a triumph in itself, although the truth lay in that Hitler was looking for a peaceful solution he thought he could better obtain if he allowed the BEF to escape.

Churchill had to admit and address the biggest issue, the equipment loss: "The best of all we had to give had gone to the British Expeditionary Force, and although they had not the numbers of tanks and some chapters of equipment which were desirable, they were a very well and finely equipped Army. They had the first-fruits of all that our industry had to give, and that is gone."

He also made it a rallying point for bringing in vast changes to war production: "An effort the like of which has never been seen in our records is now being made. Work is proceeding everywhere, night and day, Sundays and weekdays. Capital and Labour have cast aside their interests, rights, and customs and put them into the common stock. Already the flow of munitions has leaped forward. There is no reason why we should not in a few months overtake the sudden and serious loss that has come upon us, without retarding the development of our general program."

Churchill praised both the Royal Navy for running the gauntlet into the harbour and beaches and the Army for holding the perimeter through the evacuation. He pointed out the Army was saved to fight another day and that planning a defence was a priority: "We have to reconstitute and build up the British Expeditionary Force once again, under its gallant Commander-in-Chief, Lord Gort. All this is in train; but in the interval we must put our defences in this Island into such a high state of organization that the fewest possible numbers will be required to give effective security and that the largest possible potential of offensive effort may be realized."

Churchill talked up the role of RAF fighters because he knew from the strategic paper of the chiefs of staff (chapter 7), this was where the short-term investments had to be made: "The Royal Air Force engaged the main strength of the German Air Force, and inflicted upon them losses of at least four to one; and the Navy, using nearly 1,000 ships of all kinds, carried over 335,000 men, French and British, out of the jaws of death and shame, to their native land and to the tasks which lie immediately ahead."

Churchill brought the civilian population into the conflict by explaining the massive impact of civilian craft, without which the evacuation would not have been possible. The public readily identified with this, and the popular press made it central to the story.

Churchill also dispensed ideas about suing for peace and sent a clear message to fight on:

"Even though large tracts of Europe and many old and famous States have fallen or may fall into the grip of the Gestapo and all the odious apparatus of Nazi rule, we shall not flag or fail."

Churchill then went on to deliver probably the most memorable speech in British history:

"We shall go on to the end, we shall fight in France, we shall fight on the seas and oceans, we shall fight with growing confidence and growing strength in the air, we shall defend our Island, whatever the cost may be, we shall fight on the beaches, we shall fight on the landing grounds, we shall fight in the fields and in the streets, we shall fight in the hills; we shall never surrender..."[2] Parliament broke into boisterous cheers and congratulated him warmly. One member wrote to him, "That was worth a 1000 guns, and speeches of 1,000 years."[3]

In a significant lesson for today's projects, Churchill had told a story that could be related from person to person. This was a rallying cry for the nation and became a historical turning point for the British to build on the positive psychological boost that was needed. To emphasize the point that he knew the road ahead was hard, he said, "Wars are not won by evacuations."[4]

Figure 8.2. The press tried to spin Dunkirk's disaster positively. (Source: © The British Library (2006.) (Original newspaper supplied by John Frost.)

Conclusion

Churchill walked a tightrope where he could have been ejected from power following Dunkirk. Instead, he pulled off one of the most significant speeches of the whole war and that of his life. In this one speech, not only did he boost morale but also he started to set the priorities that will be examined in the next chapter. This was leadership at the finest, and Churchill's prestige, as well as his resolution to keep going, was elevated.

Key Lessons

In today's projects:

- Agile leaders are ready to discuss and communicate their response or actions in a positive manner.

  And:

- Scope Management (PMBoK KA)—

  - Keep a macro view, and remind others of it when things get off track.

- Communication Management (PMBoK KA)—

  - Be ready to communicate what the strategy is and how it leads to the project objectives.

  - Use it with the management of change process.

  - Have a project story that people can buy into and internalize.

  - Focus back on the project mantra.

  - Do not let a short-term victory en route cloud thinking.

Educators

- Discuss the importance of setting up communications strategies in today's projects. What are the most common roadblocks to this?

CHAPTER NINE

Churchill Lays Out a Strategy with Short/Long-term Objectives

This chapter looks at how Churchill laid out a strategy with short- and long-term objectives.

By June 5, Churchill had been swept up by a series of events and had to operate reactively. He had been in power for less than a month. Dunkirk, a victory grasped from the jaws of defeat, gave Churchill a small window in which to operate proactively and start to implement an overall strategy.

> **In every project, there comes a point were the PM needs to lay out a vision and bring clarity to the project.**

On the same day, the Axis forces lined up 119 divisions, including 10 armoured divisions, against the rest of France. By June 7, Allied troops fell back to a front sixty miles north of Paris. The Battle of France became a foregone conclusion. With the threat only twenty-one miles away, the United Kingdom was now the next target. Churchill warned

Parliament "invasion was a real risk to be met with total and confident defiance."[1] He was determined to fight on, but this was not going to be easy. Churchill had to identify and prioritize all the problems, lay out a strategy with short- and long-term objectives, and then develop solutions. The problems were

- With no potential allies in the Soviets who had a non-aggression pact with the Nazis, and the U.S. staunchly neutral, the fight was in one theatre.

- An invasion was likely in July to August as the United Kingdom was the last Western Ally still at war.

- The small British army was responsible for defending a very long 700-mile coastline, with no existing fortifications, little equipment, and no heavy equipment.

- The large overpopulated and vastly industrialized island had an economy on a civilian, not a war, footing.

- With the exception of coal, all raw materials were scarce, expensive (driving up the costs of production), and imported. About 67% of food was imported.

- Serious splits within the government with some senior ministers reluctant to continue fighting. Public confidence in Churchill and his project team was still very low.

- The Royal Air Force (RAF) was about 50% below its target strength and woefully behind in its ability to fend off the German Luftwaffe, having lost 509 fighters (50%) in April and May of 1940.

With 675 RAF fighters, it faced an estimated 3,500 aircraft (1,100 fighters).

- The race to reach a target (set in 1939) of 1,200 fighters was lost. Aircraft production was six months behind schedule and needed to be stepped up, but it could not possibly meet the Luftwaffe strength in time. The total United Kingdom factory output of 290 fighters per month was very low, compared to the Axis output of 500 fighters per month, and could not possibly produce enough in fighters in time for a prolonged air battle. A new Spitfire factory had been trying to get up to speed for six months, and it was still unable to meet its targets.

- An acute shortage of pilots, around 60%, meant the Force was below operational strength.

Churchill set out clear objectives, related to the problems faced, of what he had to do, what their scope was, whether they could be solved, and what resources were available.

- In the short term, he had to stave off the invasion.

- In the long term, he had to get the Americans involved in the war somehow. He could call upon no other powerful allies, as the Soviet Union and Nazis had signed a non-aggression pact.

Churchill defined a short- and long-term unified strategy to win the war. In the short term (two months):

- He had to restore confidence in his project and the will to fight on first within his cabinet, then with the government, and then with the public.

- He had to inspire his nation to continue a fight already considered lost by many, win the air battle, and stall invasion until spring 1941.

Based on everything Churchill had learned in his short time in the office, he immediately had to

1. Set up an effective project team.

2. Create an over-arching governance framework.

3. Make up for the numerical disparity in fighters by

   - Improving the supply chain, focusing on producing essentials tied to the specific demands of RAF Fighter Command.

   - Investing in emerging technologies, so RAF Fighter Command could better manage its resources.

4. Transform his organization and processes to line up behind the project.

5. Run it is an "agile" project—flexible and open to new and changing requirements.

As part of the long-term strategy (up to five to seven years), Churchill had to

- Quickly move the peacetime economy to a war footing to sustain total economic warfare.

- Expand the war through an alliance with the U.S.

- Bring hope to Nazi-occupied Europe and to the free world.

This could only be accomplished if the short-term strategy was met, which looked unlikely and against all the odds.

Churchill knew that the U.S. was an indispensable ally although not formally in the war. Churchill had to cultivate a relationship and attain Roosevelt's support.

In summary, Churchill committed himself and the nation to all-out war until victory was achieved. Behind this objective, lay his short- and long-term strategies to which he adhered with remarkable consistency throughout the war. The Axis was the enemy, and nothing would distract Churchill from leading the entire British people in defeating it. Anyone who shared this goal, even a Communist, was an acceptable ally.

"The problem is not winning the war, but persuading people to let you win it."[2]

Conclusion

Churchill used the breathing space he gained from Dunkirk to lay out a short-/long-term strategy and a vision that he immediately enabled. He now had to set up a governance framework to aid in transforming the United Kingdom.

Key Lessons

In today's projects:

- Agile leaders focus on problems ahead (prioritize these) and lay out a vision.

- Agile leaders move quickly and iteratively, with agility, once the vision is clear.

- Agile leaders look forward and position for the continual and sustained success of the organization.

- Agile leaders are focused on value-added outcomes.

- Agile leaders see beyond the short term and do not sacrifice the longer-term objectives for it.

- Agile leaders have a resilience and fortitude to stand up for what matters.

- Agile leaders define clear objectives, both short- and long-term, so the scope can be controlled and narrowed accordingly.

- Agile leaders know transformation is dynamic where the consequence of inaction is worse than action.

- Agile leaders are forward-looking, can set objectives, and have a vision of the future that can be adopted by the organization.

  And:

- Risk Management (PMBoK KA)—

  o Analyze the risks for critical activities and critical path work in the schedule to minimize impact of on-time completion.

- Integration Management (PMBoK KA)—

  o Set out short- and long-term objectives. Define a high-level plan without the details, and let the project sub-leaders develop these. Avoid a large up-front documentation effort, as this should be delivered in time.

Educators

- Discuss why Churchill defined objectives, both short- and long-term, even though he was under severe time constraints. Is this realistic in today's world?

CHAPTER TEN

Churchill Sets Up a Governance Framework

This chapter discusses how Churchill set up a governance framework to transform the United Kingdom. The term governance[1] as used in industry (especially in the information technology (IT) sector) describes the processes that need to exist for a successful project.

When Churchill became PM, he faced insistent criticism that there was no central direction of the economic effort. This was down to the flawed governance framework he inherited which consisted of disparate government, military, and civilian organizations. These well-organized and highly institutionalized structures with unique cultures acted autonomously and were used to working in their own ways. For example, the armed forces had evolved independently without a need to interface with each other, often jockeying for resources and even having their own lexicons. The Royal Navy with a five-hundred-year history considered itself the veteran, and was reluctant to cooperate closely or share resources with the British Army or its junior partner, the Royal Air Force, with a five-year history.

Churchill wrote to Eden following Dunkirk on June 6, "We are indeed the victors of a feeble and weary departmentalism."[2] This reflected the desire for change. Churchill had to rein in these organizations, particularly the military, deconstruct the vertical silos, and reconstruct a horizontal enterprise view of total warfare. He had to resist pressures and politics, prioritize the choices, and integrate these organizations to fight for a single purpose (chapter 9).

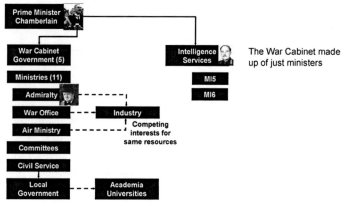

Figure 10.1. The government of Chamberlain, 1940.

To achieve the transformation, Churchill needed a governance framework that worked, not a simple task, and then to get a high degree of compliance to it. He also had to deal with adoption of his project, selling the nation, and overcoming barriers to success.

A governance framework is essential for most projects today, to guide it, particularly when the project has to work across silos or the solution is enterprise wide. Typically, the biggest problem is that of jurisdiction and boundaries. Many projects will come under the scrutiny of a body such as a Project Management Office (PMO) that provides guidance in creating a framework to set up project structure, roles, responsibilities, authority, and competencies. It also arbitrates when it overlaps with other projects.

Churchill's experience from the First World War was vital as he had been the Minister for War Production and was responsible for scaling up tank manufacturing, a technology that could have an enormous impact on the stalemate warfare of the trenches. He oversaw the production of over 350 tanks to use in the large-scale tank offensive at Cambrai with significant results. Most importantly, he had seen first-hand the importance of closely aligning industry (civilian) with military demand under government auspices.

In 1940, Churchill created four new ministries as part of his first change to the governance framework, and these were:

- Aircraft Production[3]—Churchill believed the Air Ministry had failed to meet its targets and so wanted to take aircraft manufacturing away from them. The dramatic move was in itself an indication of the commitment now set to fighter aircraft.

- Defence—this was a new post to control the course of the war and would become the focus of all efforts.

- Food Production—with the United Kingdom under siege and surrounded by a submarine blockade, this ministry would ensure the nation's food supply.

- Economic Warfare—Churchill wanted to look at all aspects of the war and for opportunities for putting pressure on the enemy, not just military means. In addition, with pressure on scarce resources and raw materials, this ministry would also examine the independent procurement processes of the armed forces.

  In addition:

- He entrenched the chiefs of staff (CoS), or the military arms, into the War Cabinet to take part in all cabinet meetings and to build up a close relationship through daily contact.

- He assumed the position of Minister of Defence to put forward suggestions that the CoS had to consider. He was always keen to listen to others' views and changed his mind if so persuaded. He had always been a channel for new ideas and projects (chapter 2).

- He diminished the role of the treasury to avoid its becoming a bottleneck and implementing financial restrictions that might compromise the short- and long-term objectives. After all, the very survival of the United Kingdom was at stake. In the previous administration, the treasury had predominance in its role.

  o Before May 1940, the government thought of "financial and economic plans" and put the accent on the first word. The new government shifted the order of words and put "economic" in front of "financial."[4]

- He had much more power than the First World War PM (Lloyd George) had and could dismiss or elevate anyone to any position. He had almost dictatorial powers over the CoS and the government, but he never overruled the CoS who always had the final say in military matters.

- He instituted two Defence Committees—one for operations, the other for supplies—both infinitely flexible bodies that endured to the end of the war.

- He reduced the number of committees that ministers were expected to attend, so they could focus on what was important.

- He introduced a new system of handling briefs and introduced "action this day," a label affixed to papers and directives.

- Appalled by the fact minutes were seldom taken, he insisted on written evidence of decisions on plan.

- The lack of good economic information aggravated one of the major limitations of central economic control. Therefore, he initiated the Economic Section of the Offices of the War Cabinet and the Central Statistical Office. For the first time, he assembled the main heads of information necessary for keeping the economic problems of war under review.

Other changes to the governance framework followed, but the significance of these initial changes was to align this to Churchill's strategy with its short- and long-term objectives.

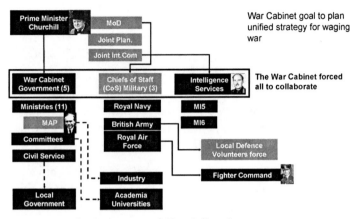

Figure 10.2: the Government of Churchill 1940.

Conclusion

Churchill started to break down barriers between vertical organizations through a revised governance framework. Churchill, with the chiefs of staff embedded in the War Cabinet, was the core of the system and a war-winning framework. The grand war strategy was run in a rational and logical way with checks and balances. It continued to evolve in 1941, but the core remained unchanged from the summer of 1940 until the war was won. Churchill's move with the treasury was not reckless but a necessity for the time, although the overall budget had to be managed carefully.

Key Lessons

In today's projects:

- Agile leaders overcome the organization's bureaucratic desire and need for stability.

- Agile leaders create fluid organizational structures with a short-term duration that can be easily modified for increased flexibility and responsiveness.

- Agile leaders create broad job descriptions to maximize flexibility where the jobs are fluid and can be substituted.

- Agile leaders are imaginative and based on the situation can make timely and appropriate changes in their thinking, plans, and methods. They encourage creative thinking of new and better goals, ideas, and solutions to problems. They reward achievement, innovation, and change.

  And:

- Human Resources Management (PMBoK KA)—

  o Set up a governance framework to enhance the project to meet the short- and long-term objectives.

  o Remove inhibitors where possible and instill concepts of agility into the framework.

Educators

- In today's world, where matrix organizations are more prevalent, discuss whether a governance framework would have as much of an impact as it did for Churchill.

- In today's world, how feasible is to promote project objectives that override cost controls?

CHAPTER ELEVEN

Churchill's Choices of What to Do (Designs a Solution)

This chapter discusses the tactical choices he made to meet the short-term objectives of his project and the initial designs of the solution.

In 1940, emerging technology had mechanized warfare (chapter 4), and agility was the new mode of operation for the military where armies could move very rapidly. With a successful combination of highly coordinated forces on sea, land, and air, the invasion of Denmark and Norway in April 1940 perfectly demonstrated agility in action. Mobile troops quickly traversed roads that were thought impossible. The Battle of Flanders in May 1940 saw armoured columns cover forty to fifty miles per day. In the air, aircraft flew multiple sorties, striking four to five times a day, and it was not single dogfights anymore, but squadron fought squadron. Fighters protected large fleets of bombers. Blitzkrieg came as a surprise to the British military that in May 1940 had fought in France with a First World War mindset. They still relied on immovable trenches and fortified defences that mobile forces rapidly overran and surrounded.

In today's world, the term agility has become extremely important in business projects and organizations. Agility in operation or organization can include the ability:

1. **To capitalize on emerging new technologies and product development**

2. **To exploit openings or new business opportunities**

3. **To put customers at the centre of a project**

4. **To create adaptive teams that respond quickly to change**

Today, organizations, through agile thinking, leadership, and projects, can introduce this kind of agility only with a flexible infrastructure.

RAF Fighter Command had the problem of having to defend a very long 700-mile coastline. The proximity of French and Belgian airfields meant Luftwaffe raids could reach British air space in ten minutes and be over London in another ten minutes. Churchill had to find a solution to offset a very agile invader. Fortunately, he now had a governance framework with which he could work. He had to make investments in RAF Fighter Command in priority over the Navy and Army. For the British public, the Royal Navy was still held in great esteem and seen as a formidable obstacle for any invader. However, recent events proved it would be rendered ineffective without adequate fighter protection, and only with massive air cover, could it prevent a sea invasion. In addition, Churchill had to override Air Ministry pressure to invest solely in RAF Bomber Command.

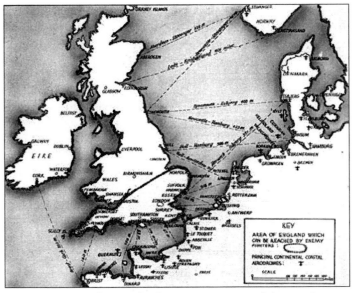

Figure 11.1. Map showing the close proximity to Axis fighters in June 1940. (Courtesy of Illustrated London News.)

Churchill brought in various scientific experts and listened to them. They presented him a few rough *technology options* that would help give RAF Fighter Command an advantage in the short term:

- The Spitfire, a modern and technically outstanding fighter, still in small numbers (33% of total fighter strength).

- Bletchley Park showed great promise in breaking the Enigma code with machines and provided critical intelligence for the Dunkirk evacuation.

- RAF Fighter Command, under the leadership of the forward thinking Air Marshal Hugh Dowding, converted a geographically distributed hierarchy and network of stations and airfields (five years old) into a headquarters at Bentley Priory.

- Radar testing proved the success of the technology in providing early warning of incoming aircraft. Churchill had supported the development of this technology in 1938, and he was involved with it while at the Admiralty (1939–1940).

- A secure, blast proof, underground facility near Downing Street with good communications.

These options were incorporated into the project to be further refined, matured, and then integrated into a solution, which would help overcome the RAF's numerical disparity with the Luftwaffe (chapter 9) because aircraft production could not meet demand in time.

As a result, Churchill took the following actions:

5. Churchill trusted his own experience from the First World War when he was Minister of Munitions responsible for tank production. There, he saw firsthand the lack of cooperation between the military and industry. He had to change that.

6. He brought in trusted lieutenants—people he knew could do the job. Foremost of those was Lord Beaverbrook, a Canadian newspaper magnate, to run fighter production and boost the output. He had closely worked with Beaverbrook over many years.

7. Lessons from the Battle of France had showed that pilots flying multiple sorties could strike many times a day magnifying the Air Force size. If the pilots could fly three to four sorties per day, then the overall number would start to match the Luftwaffe strength.

8. For a short-term solution, implementing an early warning system would improve the effectiveness

of fighters as they could be directed to specific targets. This sense-and-respond solution would be based on radar, intelligence from Bletchley Park, and a command-and-control system at Bentley Priory.

On June 14, the Axis entered Paris as Rommel's 7th Panzer Division took Le Havre. The French government left Tours for Bordeaux. Army Group C, with twenty-four divisions, prepared to cross the upper Rhine to attack the Maginot line in Alsace. All remaining British troops in France were ordered to return to England. The Battle of France was over, and the Battle of Britain would soon commence. Hence, there was little time to get the solution ready.

Conclusion

Churchill had some insight in how warfare had changed, particularly in the air, as he had been a focal point for the rearmament cause many years prior to the outbreak of war. Realizing the gap, he was more open to the use of emerging technology to make up the deficit in arms and equipment.

Key Lessons

In today's projects:

- Agile leaders, in evaluating technology options, need to be very aware of the risk and the impact on the scope, budget, and schedule.

And:

- Risk Management (PMBoK KA)—analyze the risks in all the technology options, paying close attention to emerging technologies, and for what the competition could be using these.

- Scope and Time Management (PMBoK KA)—

  o To accommodate schedules:

    - Set up deadlines for last minute scope changes.

    - Where possible, determine when scope should be culled, so deliverables can be made.

- Cost Management (PMBoK KA)—keep a very close eye on the budget when evaluating technology options.

- Human Resource Management (PMBoK KA)— for the solution, evaluate project team members for leadership roles.

Educators

- Discuss whether Churchill would have looked at emerging technologies had he not recognized the shift in warfare to mechanization and mobility. Are today's projects as open to assessing emerging technology in the early phases? What would inhibit this?

CHAPTER TWELVE

Churchill—His Background and Qualifications for Becoming a PM

This chapter discusses Churchill's background and the reasons he was so uniquely qualified to become a PM in May 1940. It looks at the skills that he brought to bear to the project. It also poses the questions of what is a good background for a PM, what are the most desired traits, and how important is previous project experience along with the battle scars?

When Churchill became PM at the ripe age of sixty-five in 1940, he had to find the strength to lead his nation forward from the darkest and most dangerous of times, towards the defeat of a tenacious enemy. Nevertheless, Churchill was ready for this, and he had always believed he had a fate with destiny that would require him to lead his nation. As he took the position, he had a very good idea of what he was undertaking with the background he had and could draw from experience in tough international negotiations or fierce political battles. In many ways, he was so well prepared that he wasted little time in taking actions.

Churchill had an extensive career that not only was in and around politics but which wove in many projects and experiences that were to prove completely invaluable. His background to 1940 included:

- 1875—Birth
- 1894—Commission for a second lieutenant in the British Army
- 1896—First book published, compiled from dispatches he wrote for a newspaper
- 1899—Reporter in Boer War (became a POW, although a non-combatant)
- 1901—Member of Parliament
- 1905—Cabinet Minister
- 1910–1911—Home Secretary
- 1911–1915—First Lord of the Admiralty
- 1915—Member of the War Council of the British Cabinet
- 1916—Commanded the 6th Royal Scots Fusiliers on the Western front
- 1917—Minister of Munitions
- 1919–1921—Secretary of State for War and Air
- 1924–1929—Chancellor of the Exchequer
- 1929–1939—Out-of-office back bencher
- 1940—Sixty-five-years old

During his career, he crashed and burned several times with unprecedented disasters, projects that would have ended anyone else's career. However, these tricky project assignments moulded him and his outlook. He was able to extract lessons and continue.

His career began as an adventurer, and with an army commission, he gained valuable military experience as an officer. After a few years, he resigned his commission to pursue a career in journalism and went out to cover the Boer War. He was captured by the Boers and imprisoned, but he managed to escape from prison, which made him a national hero.

Churchill then became a Member of Parliament and had a meteoric rise to the position of Home Secretary. In 1911, as First Lord of the Admiralty, he met with the Kaiser and moved in prestigious circles. He could take credit for preparing the British Navy for the outbreak of the First World War in 1914. He was interested in emerging technology and foresaw the use of airships (Zeppelins) for bombing raids on civilians in cities.

Figure 12.1. Churchill (First Lord of the Admiralty) with the Kaiser in 1911. (Source: Prints and Photographs Division, Library of Congress (52) LC-USZ62-75524 www.loc.gov/exhibits/churchill/wc-affairs.html.)

In 1915, as a member of the War Council of the Cabinet, Churchill suggested a plan for a new war front that would force the Germans to split their army and support the poorly rated Turkish army. However, the campaign was rapidly formulated, and the value of good intelligence, or the lack of it, and incompetent military leadership in the field led to a disastrous campaign in Gallipoli. He took the blame, and he was demoted from the Admiralty. By the end of 1915, he had resigned his cabinet post.

With his political career in tatters, Churchill embarked on the command of an infantry battalion in France, so he could look people in the eye again. He saw the horror of a static war as he fought in the trenches. From this, he clearly began to understand offense and the concept of "attack when possible"—an important mantra later on.

In 1917, Churchill was recalled to the cabinet as Minister of Munitions. For the rest of the war, he directed industrial support of the war effort by organizing the national economy for production of war materials. He was responsible for tank production and saw firsthand the lack of cooperation between military and industry, which hindered his objectives.

Through the 1930s, Churchill's party was out of office, and he held no cabinet position. However, he played a very active role in becoming a rallying point for warning the nation of the dangerous rise of German military power under the Nazi regime. This was to give him enormous credibility in 1940.

> **So, what is a good background for a PM, and how important is previous project experience along with the battle scars? A PM needs experience in similar projects relative to their selection, initiation, definition, planning, risk management, resource management, budgeting, communication, tracking issues and status, and evaluating performance.**

Churchill had experience with large-scale projects in abundance—from preparing the Navy for war, to planning the Gallipoli campaign, to coordinating the economy for the production of war materials and tanks, to running the finances of the country.

> **As well as experience, PMs require strong traits in business, technology, behaviour, and, of course, leadership skills.**

In Churchill's situation:

- He understood the challenges the United Kingdom faced better than anyone did. He had learned many lessons from the First World War, which guided his priorities in May

1940—foremost the lack of a central policy that undermined resource coordination and prolonged the United Kingdom's response.

- He was very aware of technology and could see its application in providing a clear advantage. For example, in 1915, even though he was the Lord of Admiralty, he sponsored the initial tank design. In 1938, he supported the development of radar. Although he would be involved in technical discussions, he would leave decisions to trusted lieutenants—people he knew could do the job.

- He was very perceptive in understanding human behaviour and motivating teams around him. Communication management was a cornerstone of his strategy in 1940, communicating in all directions (cabinet, government, and people) to avoid any surprises and to support the management of change process.

Churchill's leadership skills will be further discussed in chapter 27.

Conclusion

In hindsight, Churchill had an illustrious career with all the background and experience to take on the wartime PM role without actually having had a PM role. This proved to be very useful, as his people did not have an expectation in how he would play it or the outcome.

Key Lessons

In today's projects:

- Agile leaders very much leverage previous experience and refer back to it when appropriate.

- Agile leaders know that people who demonstrate agility in the field and the front line can help propagate it into the organization and drive change.

  And:

- Look back at your career and from where lessons can be brought forth.

- Risk Management (PMBoK KA)—

  o Analyze the risks in appointing a PM.

Educators

- Discuss the risks and opportunities in bringing a leader such as Churchill into the PM position. Would it be as easy to do this in today's world?

- What are the principal (three to five) ideal characteristics for leaders of transformation projects?

Agile Leadership and the Management of Change

CHAPTER THIRTEEN

Churchill's Communication Plan

This chapter discusses how Churchill put a communication plan in place to bolster morale in the government, media, and public.

Communications management is fundamental to project management in today's world (one of the nine PMBoK knowledge areas) in managing expectations. Change is constant in most projects, and as a result, constant communication is the best way to maintain connections among all the participants. Practically all projects have internal and external audiences, and importantly, the messages differ in content and tone as well as timing, for example:

- Awareness communications at the end of each project stage

- Special-purpose communications—usually a clear call-to-action

- **Data freeze communications to announce a period of no updates**
- **Launch communications to help users with new functionality**
- **Stabilization communications of resolution work for known issues**
- **Bulletin communications of changes to project dates, scope, or emerging issues, risk, or requests**

Churchill, in the early summer of 1940, had to face a series of disasters culminating with Dunkirk (chapters 8 and 9), the greatest defeat of the British army since the Napoleonic Era. Churchill, when he flew to Paris for a meeting on May 16, first learned of the full extent of the disaster that had beleaguered the French at Sedan (chapter 6) and brought the French government to near panic. Alfred Duff Cooper, at the Ministry of Information (MOI), urged Churchill to prepare the British public for bad news. Between May 10 and 14, the MOI changed news stories from Anglo-French successes in Belgium to those that indicated the possibility of defeat. Churchill and Duff Cooper, at the centre of this process, were not sure what the outcome would be so they had to be flexible and adopt different positions to accommodate ever-changing circumstances.

Figure 13.1. A montage of propaganda posters and leaflets produced by the MOI in 1940 (part of the communication plan). (Source: Unknown.)

> In today's world, a PM shapes the communications plan around the needs of each stakeholder group and plans for worst-case scenarios and crisis communications.

On May 17, newspapers openly acknowledged an Axis breakthrough on the Meuse, although editorial comment, with input from military experts, reminded readers that this had happened in March 1918, but the Allies still had won. Despite such reassurances, Churchill had designated Sunday, May 26 as a Day of National Prayer for the British Army "in peril in Flanders."

Duff Cooper implemented an effective system of news management and censoring news and found that the most effective approach was to control the source, issuing communiqués to newspapers, which editors could then interpret as they saw fit. This gave the look of diversity where, in fact, the media actually was tightly controlled.

> In today's world, project success is highly dependent on stakeholder confidence. Most PMs have faced situations where they have had to manage information to control the expectations of groups in or around the project and quell rumors that cause problems.

In 1940, the war had changed communication and the reporting of information. People were very hungry for news as everyone knew someone on the front line, but newsprint was rationed. The BBC radio news operation was rapidly expanded, and newspaper journalists were switched to radio. Incredibly, around 50% of the United Kingdom population was listening to the 9 o'clock news. For the MOI, radio presented more of a problem than newspapers. The MOI wanted to exert more control, but somehow the BBC managed to maintain a surprising degree of independence and concerned itself with telling people "how it is," no matter how gruesome the reports were. The BBC got permission to conduct radio interviews with the troops landing from Dunkirk, while newsreel cameras filmed them smiling, waving, and giving the thumbs-ups. The message was clear that the army's spirit had not been broken, even though losses on the beaches of Dunkirk were heavy.

Figure 13.2. The MOI in 1940 wanted to exert more control over the media. (Courtesy of NMSI (image 1983-5236_DHA7082).)

In today's world, PMs may have to hold back information from certain groups, in other words, control and manage who gets what and when. For example, the early results from development/testing may be poor as modules are being refined and more effort is needed. It is perfectly acceptable to keep this under wraps to maintain project morale and user confidence in a project.

Conclusion

With the role of the "little boats," Churchill and Duff Cooper had turned Dunkirk into a propaganda victory.[1] The spin was almost too successful, setting off a wave of public euphoria where a gallant loser escapes from the jaws of disaster at the very last moment. This was important, as the news was not going to get any better for a while. On June 14, the Axis marched into Paris, and for the United Kingdom who was suffering nightly bombing raids, the outlook was bleak.

Key Lessons

In today's projects:

- Agile leaders use communications proactively and extensively at all levels to support their projects and the management of change process.

- Agile leaders know communication and vision reinforcement for change are critical for enabling the transformation of the project and increasing the speed of change.

    And:

- Communication Management (PMBoK KA)—

    o Determine audience understanding of the situation and any gaps in expectations.

    o Build communication plan based on short- and long-term objectives and for addressing audience gaps.

- Risk Management (PMBoK KA)—

    o Evaluate the risks in a communication plan and strategy.

Educators

- Discuss why Churchill's communication plan proved to be so successful at Dunkirk. Were there any flaws in it? Would it work in today's business environment?

CHAPTER FOURTEEN

Churchill Personally Communicates

This chapter discusses how Churchill personally communicated using both verbal and non-verbal communication to fight the mood of defeatism, build confidence, and get buy-in into his plan.[1]

In today's world, PMs need to set up effective communication mechanisms where "effective project communications preserves your control in a project." This requires a monitoring component in the communication plan to provide feedback on the plan's effectiveness and the happenings on the ground.

Churchill's project communications were centred on radio broadcasts used to speak directly with the public. The need to keep public opinion behind the war effort and home front morale high was at the core, and he was deeply conscious of this. To get it right and to gain and sustain public confidence, he invested inordinate amounts of time. For example, he would prepare for one hour, an incredible amount of time for every minute of speech. A typical forty-minute speech would take forty hours of preparation. This is completely unrealistic for today's PM but it does put the high value of this activity into perspective.

Figure 14.1. Churchill communicating his plans. (Courtesy of the BBC.).

Churchill's schedule of broadcasts delivered a series of renowned speeches that, when all seemed lost, rallied the country to a cause. Vision and realism were central to the speeches and Churchill's gift was his ability to address his radio listeners personally, "not as unseen masses but as individuals." He envisioned his audience as a "couple and their family gathered around their coal fire in the cottage-home" and so personalized his message.

Figure 14.2. Churchill saw his audience as a "couple around their coal fire." (Source: Unknown.)

> In today's world, PMs know that project morale is essential to a working project as it can make or break it. Not all communication is verbal, actions or non-verbal communication also send out a strong message and make a statement that can be equally important to a project.

In June 1940, Churchill exemplified this approach as he recognized early on that a mood of defeatism transfixed the United Kingdom at all levels. Encouraged by the propaganda victory of Dunkirk (chapter 13), Churchill took actions to show determination to cause, instill confidence in his people, and build project morale:

- He revoked the plans to evacuate the royal family and government to Canada, where Royal Navy ships had been placed on standby.

- He ordered the disposition of great art works from the National Gallery into caves rather than being sent out of the country.

- He also discouraged the evacuation of children around the Empire—up to 6,000 children, mainly of the rich, had been evacuated.

- He stopped bombed-out theatres from being boarded up, condemning any idea that Londoners should "scuttle" the culture and arts, "that to forsake the normal routine would be an admission that the enemy had won."[2]

- He sent an edict to all civil servants to avoid defeatist talk, expecting them to set an example of "steadiness and resolution." He also encouraged the reporting of any officers "found to be consciously exercising a disturbing influence."[3]

- He stopped defeatist chatter in his cabinet and focused on changing the outlook and attitude of his ministers.

- After learning about the demoralizing effects of an air raid in the Northeast, he responded by sending a personal message to 3,000 people on the eve of an attempted invasion.

Churchill had the ability to hide his doubts and fears from the public. He stated, "One of my hardest tasks and greatest achievements was projecting confidence, even at the blackest of times."[4]

Churchill monitored the effectiveness of the plan through the following activities:

- He scoured all the newspapers every day (nine or ten) for what the population was reading, studying the editorials in detail.

- Churchill travelled and visited areas and cities that had been attacked and bombed out. Tentative at first meeting people face-to-face, he was pleasantly surprised at how well he was received, and his visits proved an enormous boost to public morale.

- The Ministry of Information carried out regular and detailed investigations into opinions, morale, and feelings of the public. The fieldworkers of mass observation were an army of mostly middle-class eavesdroppers and pub conversation listeners who reported the mood of the nation for Churchill, occasionally even with statistical estimates with a town-by-town synthesis. These were the early days of scientific polling later known as the Gallup Poll in the United Kingdom.

o The strength of these reports lay in the fact that they were compiled from a great diversity of independent sources, namely the different regional headquarters of the ministry (thirteen) and the panels of civilians and officials. The subjects were broad and covered reactions to the presentation of the war by politicians, the press, and the British Broadcasting Corporation and opinions about evacuation, housing, rationing, and strikes.

- Professor Lindemann ran Churchill's personal statistical branch with eight university statisticians made up from subject specialists. On a daily basis, this group would provide an independent assessment of any aspect of the war. This was distilled from thousands of sources of data into succinct charts and figures. Today this is known as Operations Research, used to conduct the war. This allowed Churchill to make quick decisions based on accurate data.

Figure 14.3. Professor Lindemann ran Churchill's personal statistical branch.

Conclusion

Churchill's personal communications had a significant impact on the population and further continued the positive effect from the propaganda victory at Dunkirk (chapter 13). Churchill understood building confidence in his words, "Wars are won by superior will power."[5] He also actively used the mechanism available to him to gather feedback, monitor the effectiveness of the plan, and adjust it as needed. Communications was a key part of the management of change process.

Key Lessons

In today's projects:

- "To be effective, leaders have to 'see it,' and be able to pass the vision on to every stakeholder. They must be able to tell the 'new story' if they expect their staff, constituency or clients to accept their leadership or their product."[6]

- Agile leaders at some point put a stamp of individuality on and *set the tone* for their project.

- Agile leaders continuously re-emphasize any changes and their importance, so the project team begins to accept these.

- Agile leaders should be measured on their success in bringing in the project.

  And:

- Communication Management (PMBoK KA)—

  o Closely track the morale of the project.

- o Understand audience (health) and
  expectations.

- Integration Management (PMBoK KA)—

  - o Where possible, collect data to turn into
    metrics to monitor the effectiveness of the
    plan.

Educators

- Discuss the key elements of Churchill's
  communication plan. How applicable would this
  type of plan be in today's projects?

CHAPTER FIFTEEN

Churchill Stiffens Resolve

With an invasion imminent, this chapter discusses how Churchill stiffened resolve, took the offense with decisive action, and focused on the moral dimension of events. This was very pertinent to Churchill's long-term strategy.

> **In today's world, the PM is the principal representative of the project. In many projects, after the euphoria of the kickoff meeting, there comes a point where reality sets in and so does the enormity of the task for the project team members. Confidence may start to wane and a wobble factor may creep in. The role of the PM is to act courageously to shift the mood and includes managing the project's emotional well-being.**

One of Churchill's long-term objectives (chapter 10) was to get the U.S. into an alliance with the United Kingdom and eventually involved in the war. He sent telegrams to President Roosevelt asking for support, outlining the perilous situation. He also sent telegrams to Canadian Prime Minister Mackenzie King to enlist his support and impress Churchill's case to Roosevelt. Churchill recognized the problem that Roosevelt had in supporting the United Kingdom publicly with the U.S. staunchly neutral, although in private, he encouraged Churchill.

Churchill's ability to rouse the public spirit stiffened resolve. His speeches were not just directed at the British public. He deliberately drew U.S. attention to the United Kingdom's predicament showing the world that the United Kingdom was not defeated and ready and able for a fight. In London, he courted U.S. journalists, spending his precious time on lunches with them, so they would support the United Kingdom morally and take a sympathetic stance. He gradually drew the U.S. public into supporting the United Kingdom morally.

"The verdicts of leading British newspapers, the *Daily Mail* ('grand') and the *Guardian* ('brilliantly exciting'), were shared by listeners in America—no bad thing at a time when Britain was trying to engage U.S. support."[1]

Figure 15.1. Churchill courted Roosevelt publicly. (Courtesy of Library of Congress.)

At Oran, Churchill took the most pivotal actions, which did more than anything else to convince world opinion that he was serious about the war. On July 3, the French Admiral Gensoul was offered choices to ensure his fleet with its four capital ships stayed out of Axis hands. All were turned down, and the Royal Navy opened fire on the anchored ships. Three ships were badly damaged, and one blew up. In British eyes, the Royal Navy had carried out an unhappy, but necessary, duty against their former French allies. French anger and bitterness was understandably considerable, "a hateful decision but no act more necessary..."[2] The event showed Churchill's ruthless determination to cause. It also impressed on Roosevelt that Churchill was a man of action and not bluster.

Figure 15.2. At Oran, Churchill took pivotal actions to show he was serious about the war.

Churchill inspired a resolve in the public to continue with his unending hatred and stubborn will to defeat the Axis, no matter the cost. With defeat a strong possibility, Churchill's greatest achievement was that he refused to capitulate, and he remained a strong opponent of any negotiations with the Axis. In the cabinet, few others had this degree of resolve. He also used his speeches to manage public expectations, not only preparing for the worst but to get *buy-in* for his strategy. For example, Dunkirk the disaster was turned into a victory.

In today's world, to stiffen project resolve, strong decisive action is required from the PM to get buy-in for the long term.

Churchill with decisive action proactively took the offense. In June 1940, he pointed out that in the defensive state of mind created by the Dunkirk evacuation (chapter 9) and by the possibility of an invasion, the country (public) might suffer from "the mental and moral prostration to the will and initiative of the enemy, which had ruined the French."[3] He recommended an "Attack when possible" philosophy, that is, repeated small-scale inroads on the Continent. He called for the organization of commandos to raid enemy and occupied lands. In the Middle East, the order was to drive the Axis forces out of East and North Africa and not to sit tight in Egypt.

With the continent of Europe occupied, all hopes of decisive operations by land were abandoned. For Churchill and his advisers, the time of preparations was to be given over to a long-range attack against the Axis power. The only means of attack was indirect through air bombardment, blockade, and with organized risings in the occupied territories. In the words of the chiefs of staff, immediate action should be to "destroy all upon which the German war machine rests—the economy which feeds it, the civilian morale which sustains it, the supplies which nourish it and hopes of victory which give it courage."[4]

Churchill was surprisingly willing to sacrifice any national custom social convention, military etiquette, or tradition for victory. To Churchill, nothing was sacred, and everything was open game. Parliament passed legislation placing all "persons, their services and their property at the disposal of the Crown."[5] This granted the government the most sweeping emergency powers in modern British history.

Churchill described the moral dimension of events. Churchill stated, "War is terrible but slavery is worse." He talked about the tyranny of the Nazi regime openly as threatening all that is sacred to man. He targeted his speeches at the nations of Europe, under Nazi occupation, to inspire hope, "But if we fail, then the whole world—Will sink into the abyss of a new Dark Age made more sinister, and perhaps more protracted, by the lights of perverted science."[6] He even wrote to Stalin on June 25, outlining the dangers of a Nazi-dominated Europe.

Conclusion

Churchill's greatest personal achievements were resolve to the cause and projecting confidence at a point when many people were ready to give up. He did this not just through his speeches but also his actions, most spectacularly at Oran where he took the most pivotal actions. In other words, he acted courageously to shift the mood. History was on his side, as not since the Norman invasion of 1066 had Britain been invaded and conquered.

Key Lessons

In today's projects:

- Agile leaders communicate on all levels to inform the client, the project team, and the project sponsor about the project.

- Agile leaders take calculated risks in meeting objectives.

- Agile leaders need to remind the organization that the transformation is a dynamic journey.

- Agile leaders introduce a personal element when they communicate to bring realism to the vision and the project.

- Agile leaders are inspiring, willing to take risks, and display confidence in all that they do.

  And:

- Human Resource Management (PMBoK KA)—

  o Know how far an organization can be pushed, where the resistance will come, and what can be sacrificed (As-Is) practices.

- Risk Management (PMBoK KA)—

  o Evaluate the risk in an activity and its impact on other PMBoK areas, e.g., Churchill's Oran decision, risky as it was, had a great impact in augmenting his long-term goal and his communication strategy.

- Communication Management (PMBoK KA)—

  o When the going gets tough, or if the project "wobbles," refer to the communication strategy in determining how to restore confidence.

Educators

- Discuss Churchill's decision at Oran, and determine its importance to supporting his longer-term strategy.

- Could taking such dramatic actions work in today's business environment?

CHAPTER SIXTEEN

Churchill's Team

This chapter switches gears and looks at how Churchill's organization prepared itself for the air battle to meet his short-term objectives of staving off the invasion of the United Kingdom.

For Churchill, radio broadcasts were the core of his project communications and used to promote his strategy (chapter 10). Combined with his governance framework (chapter 11), this would allow his organization to pursue the complex project, the single objective of which was the survival of the United Kingdom in the short term. The successes of his public communications after Dunkirk (chapter 14) took the pressure off him and his team to execute the project.

The project would span the breadth of the United Kingdom and touch the British establishment, government, industry, armed forces, society, and economy. Churchill threw everything behind the project that would deliver a solution (chapter 11) to ramp up the capabilities of the much-depleted Royal Air Force (RAF) Fighter Command squadrons. The solution consisted of four areas:

- The first, *the "fighter" supply chain*, focused on supplying the essentials to meet the specific demands of RAF Fighter Command—from the gathering of vital raw materials, transporting these, and prioritizing their use to the most critical factories related to fighter production. In parallel, a reorganization of the labour force ensured the labour with the right skills to run the *supply chain*.

- The second related to amassing information on enemy activities, *creating intelligence and ultimately knowledge*. It could also provide feedback from collecting data after actions were taken to determine the impact of these.

- The third related to investing in emerging technologies so that RAF Fighter Command could *better manage its resources*, specifically its pilots and fighters. The output would be an integrated air defence system, a sense-and-respond system, with a complex decision-making environment at its centre.

- The fourth was a *command centre* and Executive Dashboard for Churchill, his inner government, and chiefs of staff. It was a principal facility and community that made the overriding decisions that affected the other areas.

In today's projects, establishing the right mix in the project team is a prerequisite for success. A good team is a prerequisite to a successful project. Every PM knows that people make or break a project. Looking for skill sets is just part of the search, just as important are leadership and personalities for the team leader roles that will help install confidence and rally support for the project. Yet, in a recent study, only 41% of project managers engage senior management and/or sponsor support to build their team, and as few as 6% fight to get the best people on their projects.

Churchill needed leaders and visionaries that could cut through the red tape of bureaucracy for this project to be successful. He saw the mistakes of the First World War where the government had failed to coordinate the war effort centrally. He created a National Government or *Grand Coalition* so as not to repeat these mistakes and brought the *best-qualified* members into the highest positions. To the annoyance of his supporters, he kept in adversaries such as Chamberlain and Halifax to unify his War Cabinet and strengthen national confidence. He also knew an "outcast" could become a "focus for negotiating discontents" with the war. "Better in than out" and "let bygones be bygones," were magnanimous gestures.

Churchill knew what problems had to be addressed. He had the power to appoint or dismiss everyone and used this power readily. As a PM, he had to make sure he had the right leaders in place to be able to pull the teams together:

- First, Churchill appointed Max Aitken (Lord Beaverbrook, see figure 16.1 below), a Canadian newspaper magnate, to run the fighter supply chain at the newly formed Ministry of Air Production. He was Churchill's confidante, friend, industrialist, and a no-nonsense newspaper baron. It was significant because he was given the mandate to cut through the red tape.

- Second, the Secret Intelligence Service (SIS) had Stewart Menzies at its head. Appointed Chief of SIS in 1939, he was responsible for wartime intelligence and counterintelligence departments and the fledgling code breaking efforts at Bletchley Park. He became Churchill's master spy chief.

- Third, RAF Fighter Command had Hugh Dowding, who had helped establish it in 1935, at its helm. Dowding was seen as difficult and remote, but in reality, he was very focused on objectives and very close to his crews and pilots. Although some wanted to remove Dowding, Churchill told his Air Minister, "I think he is one of the very best men you have got... he has my full confidence."[1] When Dowding presented the case not to send any more fighters to France, Churchill, after deliberation, supported him.

- Fourth, the command centre had Churchill at its head. He appointed himself minister in the newly created Ministry of Defence (chapter 11) so that he would be in a position to put forward suggestions that had to be considered by the CoS and control the course of the war.

Figure 16.1. Max Aitken pictured on Time magazine, September 16, 1940. (Courtesy of Time Inc.)

Conclusion

One of the characteristics of these men was their ability to stand up to Churchill and challenge him. This provided the checks and balances necessary in a well-rounded organization and created a mutual respect.

In today's projects, specifically those that span across organizational boundaries, finding the right mix of people for the project team is a prerequisite for success. Often players from across the organization are needed to help with adoption and buy-in.

Key Lessons

In today's projects:

- Agile leaders set up authority but do not rely on it. Greater influence is accorded to people who demonstrate the ability to add value.

- Agile leaders look for leaders that can challenge the status quo and are unafraid of going out on a limb.

- Agile leaders are broad-minded and seek out adversity of viewpoints and opinions.

  And:

- Human Resource Management (PMBoK KA)—

  o Evaluate project sub teams (As-Is) to develop a balance of As-Is and To-Be project staff.

  o Find leaders with right characteristics for the sub project teams.

  o Find internal change agents among the operation's regular members to promote the merits of the change. These are highly regarded, convince sceptics, and lead teams.

- Risk Management (PMBoK KA)—

  o Minimize the risk by using proven talent and people with a record of accomplishment.

Educators

- Discuss the pros and cons of bringing in your own team—known players—into a project.

- How do you handle potential project adversaries and competitors?

CHAPTER SEVENTEEN

The "Fighter" Supply Chain

This chapter looks at how Beaverbrook and his leadership style made an immediate impact on the Ministry of Aircraft production (MAP) and how the concepts of supply chain agility, just-in-time manufacturing, and zero inventories were introduced to offset a pending disaster.

In the last two weeks of May 1940, the Royal Air Force (RAF) sustained massive losses of close to 500 operational fighters in the air battle over Flanders and France. Winston Churchill was now facing the prospects of an imminent invasion. With 620 operational fighters, the RAF was well below its set target (in 1939) of 1,200 fighters, thought to be the minimum number to win an air battle over the United Kingdom. The fighters were outnumbered by a ratio of 2:1, and the RAF was about 50% under strength with very little time to increase manufacturing output. The fighter production rate was still struggling to meet targets of 200 fighters per month. Even the boost of a new Spitfire fighter factory, plagued by the complexity of the Spitfire's elliptical wings, had failed to produce anything in six months.

Figure 17.1. Spitfire's elliptical wings caused production problems. (Courtesy of Crown copyright.)

In May 1940, as the British army was evacuated from Dunkirk, Prime Minister Winston Churchill faced a disaster and asked his chiefs of staff to report on the problem of the defence of the United Kingdom. The report stressed the overwhelming superiority of the enemy on land and in the air. The United Kingdom was forced into a defensive strategy until the deficits in labour and equipment could be made up. This would mean a relatively long wait of two or three years.

Churchill had to respond to the invasion threat and jump-start fighter production immediately. The problem was that the United Kingdom economy, in spite of everything, was on a civilian footing. Household goods and new automobiles were still being built and diverting critical manufacturing resources and raw materials. Churchill had to prioritize fighter production over everything, even bomber production that the Air Ministry had been prioritizing.

Changes in the Governance Framework

One of the earliest and most important decisions by Churchill in the running of war production was the formation of a new ministry namely the Ministry of Aircraft Production. Churchill believed the Air Ministry had failed to meet its fighter production targets and had to be replaced. The dramatic move was in itself an indication of the commitment now set to fighter aircraft and the urgency that was now attached to it.

Churchill needed a strong leader that could turn around fighter production. Churchill appointed Canadian Lord Beaverbrook, a close confidante he had known since they both served in the First World War cabinet of Lloyd George, as its minister. Churchill could trust him and gave him a clear mandate to transform fighter production. Beaverbrook, a newspaper magnate, was a no-nonsense man who could cut through the red tape of government bureaucracy. He was an outsider who would take a very different approach to accelerate production and to the supply chain to lock step it to the daily demands of RAF Fighter Command. This was one of the earliest and most important decisions by Churchill in the running of war production.

Figure 17.2. The Ministry of Aircraft Production took over production in May 1940. (Courtesy of Crown copyright.)

Beaverbrook thought that the Air Ministry was not well suited to running aircraft production and that people he described as *air marshals* were not appropriate by character or training. He envisioned making his ministry into a fast-growing enterprise run by business people who, in Beaverbrook's words, "knew what they were doing." They had the business background and an administrative approach that was more spontaneous and informal than the established practices of government departments. The latter was grounded in red tape, routine, paperwork, or, as Beaverbrook put it, "organization was the enemy of improvisation."[1] They could better adapt to what was required in modern fighter production.

Beaverbrook reasoned that even if this existed at the lower levels of the ministry pyramid, the top levels would be run by an informal group of his personal advisers drawn from business and industry, with Mr. Hennessy of Ford Motors at its head. This reflected how best practices were brought in from the automobile[2] manufacturing industry to speed up fighter production. In a short time, the ministry closely reflected the personality of Beaverbrook and the critical urgency of the tasks he had to face.

Figure 17.3. Hawker Kingston Plant. (Courtesy of Crown copyright.)

Beaverbrook was aware that the average life of a fighter in war was two months, and with a fighter force of thirty-four squadrons, industry would need to produce 350 new aircraft a month just to maintain front-line strength. Although battle losses could be replaced from manufacturing, reserves, or repair, Beaverbrook recognized that even with major increases in production likely, losses would out strip these. As a result, Beaverbrook had to approach the problem with out-of-the-box thinking, and he instituted or supported the following initiatives:

- Because of the acute shortage of workers as the military draft took its toll:

    o The Minister of Labour, Ernest Bevin, ended the poaching of skilled workers by rival employers. The Restriction on Engagement Order of June 1940 made it compulsory for recruitment to occur only through employment exchanges. As a result, thousands of workers were directed out of civil industries into war production such as fighters.

- o Out of every nine in the work force, two were in the armed services and three in war production.

- o Women were encouraged through an extensive promotion campaign to enter the workforce in large numbers to fill the gaps created by military conscription.

- A strategy that promoted production at the expense of all other activity, including spare parts production, today known as zero inventory.

- Agreement that, at least until the end of September 1940, all efforts were to be concentrated on the production of just Hurricanes and Spitfires with fighters having higher priority over bombers. If it was profitable, then labour from other aircraft factories was to be transferred over as well.

Beaverbrook introduced the concepts of supply-chain agility: standardization, simplification, modularity, and integration to improve the efficiency of the supply chain:

- The supply chain was revamped to improve agility and speed up delivery output. Production of fighters was limited from five to two proven types—the Hurricane and Spitfire, which were already in quantity production. Fewer aircraft types left in production eliminated some business processes. *Standardization* provided everything needed for Hurricane and Spitfire production so it could be immediately stepped up. Standardization safeguarded the supply of materials and equipment already allocated for these types and made it possible to divert from other types the necessary parts, stocks of materials and components, and reserves of production capacity for immediate use. Aircraft parts were sourced from hundreds of large and small suppliers to ensure availability and a continuous flow and avoid bottlenecks.

- Fighter production was *simplified* by reducing the number of small and disparate components by concentrating on completed subassemblies (fuselage frames, undercarriages, instrument panels, engines) shipped straight from suppliers. This reduced complexity in business process execution.

- Expertise and best practices were brought in from the automobile manufacturing industry to speed up fighter production. *Modularity* was introduced where reusable parts and subassemblies could be redeployed from bomber production. These could be switched back with changing needs after the air battle. Thus, the parts and subassemblies were decoupled from physical linkages to the business processes.

- Business processes were mapped out and infrastructure components for fighter production were connected. This better understanding of the production process allowed the production line to be broken out from large-scale factories to much smaller facilities such as garages that could be dispersed across geographic locations, creating a network of *integrated* manufacturing. This was useful as all fighter production facilities were top priority targets for the Luftwaffe. In addition, new processes were introduced that eliminated the elliptical wing production problems.

- The Civilian Repair Organization (CRO) was put into operation in January 1940 to recover downed pilots and aircraft. Using small civilian workshops and garages, recovered aircraft were either immediately repaired or cannibalized for spare parts. Initially, Lord Nuffield created a chain of repair shops on RAF airfields, civil aerodromes, garages, and large factory areas across the United Kingdom. Automotive engineers switched from automobile to aircraft manufacture and, along with bodywork repairers, repaired damaged aircraft, piecing together one good aircraft from two or three write-offs. Repairs were undertaken at a phenomenal rate, within twenty-four hours, where the pilot waited for the plane and would fly it back to base almost the same day straight into the battle. These were known as "fly-in" repairs and the "out-patients department." In such a lean operation, even enemy planes were salvaged and thrown into smelters to provide raw materials for new fighters.

- Further, Beaverbrook, a Canadian, had good relationships with industrialists in the U.S. and leveraged these to secure supplies of precious raw materials, key parts, and subassemblies. This outset of the transatlantic supply chain ran the course of World War II. He helped set up a system of procurement management that was the foundation for the rest of the war.

Figure 17.4. Beaverbrook instituted the concepts of supply-chain agility: standardization, simplification, modularity, and integration. (Courtesy of Birmingham City Council.)

Beaverbrook also instituted some out-of-the-box thinking:

- Spitfire funds where an individual, organization, or town could absorb the cost of an airframe (for a Spitfire, this was set at £5,000 ($20,000) although the real cost was nearer £12,000 ($48,000, or equivalent to £200,000 today)), and an aircraft would be allocated to bear the name of the donor on the fuselage. The idea of donation caught on, and Beaverbrook organized the project on an industrial scale. Many towns and organizations, joined by counterparts in the dominions and colonies, as well as other countries around the world, started to raise funds quickly. Eventually, there were around 1500 presentation Spitfires or 17% of the total production.

Figure 17.5. Beaverbrook instituted Spitfire funds supported by the dominions and colonies. (Courtesy of Science & Society Picture Library.)

Figure 17.6. Beaverbrook instituted Spitfire funds supported by organizations and business. (Courtesy of Science & Society Picture Library.)

- An aluminium appeal that promoted people to save their old pots, pans, kettles, and metal appliances and donate these to the government. Posters were printed and newspapers ran advertisements asking for old scrap metal to build fighter planes. In reality, very little was ever used in aircraft construction, but it boosted people's morale by feeling the satisfaction that they were "doing their bit." This was part of a concerted effort to get people more involved.

Figure 17.7. Beaverbrook's Aluminium Appeal. (Courtesy of Kent Messenger Group Newspapers.)

"The work you do this week fortifies and strengthens the front of battle next week... The production you pour out of your factories this week will be hurled into desperate struggle next week." [3]

Beaverbrook's Achievements

Beaverbrook effectively evolved the supply chain, introducing redundancy in the supply and a better visibility into the demand.

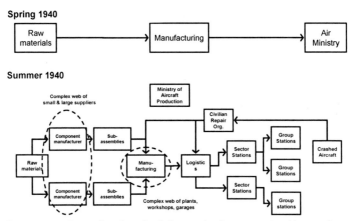

Figure 17.8. Beaverbrook evolved the supply chain considerably in a few months.

As a result, by the end of May, fighter production hit 325 fighters in one month as Beaverbrook's changes began to bite. By mid-June, a spare parts inventory secretly run by the Air Ministry was brought to Beaverbrook's attention. Following an internal battle, Beaverbrook ordered its immediate seizure and the parts put back into fighter production, as he mandated zero inventories. The whole supply chain held absolute minimum inventory to maximize the number of fighters available.

Nothing stood in the way of Beaverbrook's reorganization, and specifically, financial considerations were not allowed to impede the program. The functions of the Ministry of Aircraft Production expanded to embrace such diverse tasks as labour, construction, regional services, and aircraft distribution to sector airfields. This also included the defence of factories with anti-aircraft batteries. In addition, Beaverbrook was in close contact with Bentley Priory Fighter Command (Air Marshal Sir Hugh Dowding) and Storey's Gate, Churchill's headquarters.

Adopting New Methods

In this period, the other government production departments had escaped the major overhauls of the Ministry of Aircraft Production. They all faced change, but it came in smaller and more agreeable doses and thus evaded serious internal unsettlement. They had to undertake the duties of industrial administration new to government officials and to tackle emergencies at a quickened pace of improvisation and recruit from the business world.

Beaverbrook's approach to the supply chain was badly needed in the summer of 1940, but it distorted the supply system of the war economy. After the Battle of Britain, it was replaced by a quota system, where each ministry was allocated a quota of raw material imports based on its priority in the war effort. By the winter of 1940–41, the urgency was truly over, and in the summer of 1941, when Beaverbrook was transferred to the Ministry of Supply, the Ministry of Aircraft Production was brought into line again with the methods of the other ministries.

In summary, the Battle of Britain not only tested the pilots, their planes, and tactics, but most importantly, it was also an attritional struggle that tested the supply chains of the air forces and the production, storage, repair, and salvage of fighters.

In today's world, what can we take away from this lesson from history? Churchill had a very clear view of the situation he faced and therefore was able to prioritize his objectives and shut down non-essential war production. He was able to narrow in on fighter production and make it a priority, assigning a leader that could turn it around. Beaverbrook, an outsider, took a very different approach to the supply chain and introduced the basic concepts of agility. He mandated zero inventories to maximize the output and stuck to his principles, exceeding all expectations. Beaverbrook's supply chain was a significant factor in the story of the conflict.

> As pointed out in "The project manager is in a position to pull the management team together and rally them around the project. This can be done through exemplary behavior as a (project) manager and by focusing (the team) very closely on the project."[4]

Conclusion

In today's projects, some areas of the business will need a radical approach in improving efficiencies. Beaverbrook, an outsider, took a very different approach to the supply chain and introduced the basic concepts of agility. Beaverbrook's approach aimed to solve the problems holistically by bringing in qualified industry leaders, securing raw materials, resolving labour issues, and building public good will. Churchill's selection of a hard-nosed leader such as Beaverbrook was well justified.

Key Lessons

In today's projects:

- Agile leaders:
  - Continuously challenge preconceived notions.
  - Control the project scope, so it can be narrowed and delivered through iterations to show progress.

- Consider and introduce best practices from cross industry.

- Pay great attention to human resource pools—in acquiring them and their development.

- Monitor staff movement to ensure critical personnel are not transferred from a critical activity to another part of the project.

- Analyze staffing levels versus the schedule frequently (weekly) to ensure that sufficient labour is available to complete work on the critical path while also reallocating excess labour to control costs.

- Monitor for hoarding of skilled staff where project leaders are responsible for meeting individual schedules and goals.

- Select leaders based on their ability to cut through red tape.

And:

- Scope Management (PMBoK KA)—

  - Determine the business processes that need to go through the transformation.

- Procure Management (PMBoK KA)—

  - Reduce the risks of undersupply by sourcing from several vendors.

  - Build relationships early.

  - Avoid creating potential bottlenecks.

- Human Resource Management (PMBoK KA)—

  - Select for key positions the best people with a proven record of accomplishment.

- Spend time evaluating staff and their skill sets available to the project.
- Time Management (PMBoK KA)—
  - Ensure planning activities are not overly broad in scope so
    - They are difficult to measure and estimate with confidence.
    - They can mask details that can be overlooked.
    - They can make the schedule difficult to achieve.
- Quality Management (PMBoK KA)—
  - Ensure quality planning is considered, as this issue usually is poorly addressed in situations with a short time line or in a chaotic state.

Educators

- Discuss the impact of Beaverbrook's outside view on the project. How would this approach work in today's projects?
- Discuss the merits of
  - Using cross-industry practices
  - Introducing peripheral schemes in relation to the core business

Creating Intelligence and Knowledge

This chapter looks at the second area of the overall project—the mechanization and automation of the production of intelligence.

"Knowledge is power"—a recent quote, or is it? Well, actually, Sir Francis Bacon, English author, courtier, and philosopher, made it in 1597. In the military, knowledge has always been important, especially in decision making. In recent decades, knowledge, or *intelligence*, has emerged as one of the most vital military assets. Although we may perceive the concept of military intelligence as old as warfare itself, this chapter presents an example of the industrial production of it back in May 1940 to respond to the demands of a nation in crisis. This was the first real concerted effort into the production of intelligence through the introduction of mechanization and a level of automation. Electro-mechanical computers would support the process of information gathering, collection, collation, deciphering, and interpretation. Bletchley Park revolutionized modern warfare within an incredibly short period and the manner in which air wars were going to be conducted from that point on.

Churchill had to use the limited resources he had at his disposal in the most effective way. He could only do that through the greater use of organizational and enemy intelligence. Knowing the extent of enemy preparation and activity would provide the necessary insight to where and how the enemy was likely to strike next. Armed with this, Churchill could then better target resources to meet the invasion threat.

Shaped by his previous experiences from the First World War, Churchill knew the value of intelligence. First, the lack of a central policy undermined coordination of resources and prolonged the United Kingdom's response and the war. Second, the lack of reliable intelligence proved a major undoing for him at Gallipoli in 1915 and curtailed his career short term. Churchill's plan to defeat Turkey out of the war by sending in British warships and troops to stand off Constantinople failed miserably. At Gallipoli, the troops hit the beaches without adequate ground intelligence. They did not have anywhere to hide, and the Turkish army that commanded the heights and overall terrain of the beaches gunned them down.

As Churchill came to power in May 1940, he was made aware of the secret establishment at Bletchley Park that collected and deciphered encrypted enemy communications or Enigma codes under the overall command of Stewart Menzies, the Director of Military Intelligence (MI6). Bletchley Park was opened in 1938 when the Government Codes & Ciphers School was moved there to test its suitability for warfare. The mansion (see figure 18.1) was located midway between the Universities of Oxford and Cambridge, a fertile community and source of mathematicians and logicians—all ideal code-breaker candidates.

Figure 18.1. Bletchley Park Mansion. (Courtesy of Bletchley Park Trust.)

The first breakthrough for Bletchley Park came in July 1939 when Polish cryptographers shared their Enigma work and results with the French and British. They had obtained examples of the commercial Enigma machine and managed to break the codes. They also had an idea for developing a mechanical method for finding the Enigma ring settings to speed up deciphering. The Polish work gave the Bletchley organization a great boost, and in January 1940, Hut 6 code breakers made their first break into Enigma. However, the operation was still fledgling and manual, very laborious, and it was hit-and-miss whether the messages could be deciphered before an event would actually happen. An electro-mechanical machine could greatly reduce the odds, and thereby the time required, to break the daily-changing Enigma keys. Work started on this under the leadership of the renowned Alan Turing (father of the Turing Machine and pioneer of computing)

Figure 18.2. Enigma code.

In May 1940, during the Battle of France, the value of deciphered enemy communications, especially from the German Army when field commanders filed situation reports to headquarters each day, started to emerge,. This allowed the British commanders to check on their own information and build up a more accurate intelligence picture. This gave great confidence in the potential of intelligence and greatly raised Bletchley's profile with the military.

Several new prototypes of electro-mechanical machines (bombes) (see figure 18.3) were completed in May 1940, based on the original Polish idea, and initial results proved very promising as the operation of deciphering was dramatically sped up. If messages were decrypted in a twenty-four-hour window, this would provide invaluable information on enemy intent and threats and allow defensive positions to be taken prior to any enemy offensive. Considered highly secure by the Axis, the odds against breaking Enigma were a staggering 150 million million million to one, so it was unlikely this source of intelligence would come under suspicion.

Figure 18.3. Electro-mechanical machines (bombes) helped in automation. (Photo Credit: National Security Agency.)

As Churchill quickly recognized the potential at Bletchley, the necessary investments were made to automate and scale up the operation further. This was done through the influx of skilled staff and more bombes into Hut 3, which dramatically optimized the operation. The operation was given the code name "Ultra," and then shrouded in a veil of security. A network of listening stations ("Y" stations) (see figure 4) was set up to gather raw wireless signals for processing at Bletchley. The focus at Bletchley was not just on breaking the Enigma code. As the volume of messages increased, a significance or priority was placed on key messages going to chiefs of staff and Churchill. This proved extremely valuable for the recipients. However, a new cog in the operation was required, namely an interpretation unit known as the Shadow OKH (German Army High Command) in Hut 3, which required the influx of skilled interpreters. The emphasis was on pooling this information with previous messages to create an enormous bank of organized knowledge.

As a result, of these initiatives:

- An elaborate level of security was developed to protect Ultra. Special liaison units were set up to ensure that Ultra was only put into the hands of a few key decision-makers to lower the risk of the Axis discovering the source of the intelligence.

- Ultra intelligence and knowledge could be applied to decision making, specifically in the War Cabinet and in a limited form in RAF Fighter Command.

- Ultra could give Dowding[1] details of the Luftwaffe order of battle down to individual commanders in the field. The output framed the messages in the larger context of what was happening on the enemy front.

- Churchill took a deep personal interest in Bletchley and described it as "the goose that laid the golden egg, but didn't cackle."[2]

- To help ensure that Ultra was being used effectively, Churchill introduced the systematic use of it across his enterprise (all three military arms). In some situations, he was outraged when his commanders did not use it.

- An elaborate decoy system was set up so if actions resulted from Ultra, the Axis had to be fooled into thinking that the source of intelligence came from elsewhere but Ultra.

- Ultra was arguably the first concerted efforts to introduce Knowledge Management on such a large scale.

- Intelligence gathering was expanded through occupied Europe.

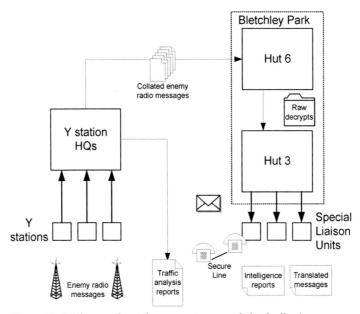

Figure 18.4. The complete Ultra operation provided a feedback mechanism.

Conclusion

In the short term, Ultra had a profound effect on the United Kingdom's defence strategies and the course of the Battle of Britain by providing early warning of enemy intent, strength, size of raids, and their timing. In the longer term, the overall knowledge-driven culture created at Bletchley Park had a profound effect on the course of the war. The military adapted to this extraordinary source of information and learned to use it with increasing effectiveness and results.

Churchill took a holistic view of the United Kingdom's resources during the war; where intelligence and process integration were clearly greater than the sum of its parts. For Churchill, "knowledge was [indeed] power," and Bletchley Park provided priceless insights into the strategic thinking and tactical intent of the enemy. In a short time, Bletchley Park [3] revolutionized warfare and the manner in which air wars were going to be fought from that point on.

Key Lessons

In today's projects:

- Agile leaders readily evaluate and innovate the technology to be part of the solution.

- Agile leaders understand the risks associated with a solution and mitigate these.

- Agile leaders make critical information widely available to permit more opportunities for more people to add value.

    And:

- Weigh up technology options and then invest accordingly for maximum return.

- Determine whether technologies need to go through a Proof-of-Concept (possibly a throwaway) to assess them thoroughly.

- Field test to provide feedback and refinements.

- Risk Management (PMBoK KA)—

    o Assess the risks in the use of intelligence and possible counter productivity.

- Human Resource Management (PMBoK KA)—

    o Extend the reach of the project to where you are likely to find pools of right skilled people, so they can be readily incorporated into it.

Educators

- Discuss the use of competitive intelligence (different categories) and the boundaries of what is ethical in today's business environment. Would it necessitate an elaborate decoy system to mask resulting actions?

CHAPTER NINETEEN

RAF Fighter Command

This chapter looks at the third area, RAF Fighter Command, and how the clever use of emerging technologies and re-engineered processes could better maximize the effectiveness of pilots/fighters in an integrated air defence or sense-and-respond system.

In June 1940, despite Air Marshal Hugh Dowding's best efforts, RAF Fighter Command was facing a major challenge. In the last two weeks of May 1940, the RAF sustained massive losses of close to 500 operational fighters[1] in the air battle over Flanders and France. With 620 operational fighters, the RAF was about 50% below its set target (in 1939) of 1,200 fighters, thought to be the minimum number to win an air battle over the United Kingdom. The fighters were outnumbered by a ratio of 2:1, and Dowding had to manage the remaining numbers of fighters very carefully, in how he deployed them in the forthcoming battle.

Dowding's Preparation

To better understand how Dowding was able to go into an air battle against such bad odds, we need to go back to 12

July 1936 and the birth of RAF Fighter Command and look at the evolution of this organization. Dowding formed his headquarters at Bentley Priory (Stanmore, Middlesex) where he was the first commander-in-chief. He had great determination and foresight in fighting the "old guard" of senior military chiefs and politicians who wanted to equip the new RAF with inexpensive and well-tried string-and-canvas biplanes. Fortunately, Dowding won and specified a design to British industry that could take off from a grass field. Eventually, he obtained high-performance heavily armed monoplanes, taken from R. J. Mitchell's S6b floatplane that had won the final three Schneider Trophy races in 1931. In 1935, the Hurricane flew, and a few months later, the prototype Spitfire came.

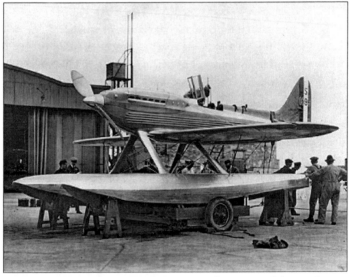

Figure 19.1. R. J. Mitchell's S6b floatplane, forerunner of the Spitfire. (Courtesy of Crown copyright.)

Dowding wanted the aircraft to be armed with heavy wing-mounted cannons and the cockpits fitted with armour plating and bulletproof glass to protect his pilots—forward thinking for the time. Despite strong opposition, he later got these, once the need was proven in battle.

Dowding was aware that the Air Ministry was very slow in scaling up its fighter production schedule and unlikely to reach the minimum target number of squadrons for many years. Therefore, he looked to other means to assist his fighters in an air battle. In 1935, he asked Watson-Watt to follow a line of research that led to the world's first operative radar network called Chain Home, which became operational in 1937.

Figure 19.2. Radar towers—the eyes of the system. (Courtesy of Crown copyright.)

Radar testing proved the success of the technology in providing early warning of incoming aircraft detected at ranges of eighty miles.

Figure 19.3. Radar network of towers along the coast. (Courtesy of Crown copyright.)

In 1936, the Observer Corps became part of the newly formed Fighter Command under Dowding and moved its headquarters to RAF Bentley Priory. This defence warning organization provided a system for detecting, tracking, and reporting aircraft over the United Kingdom.

Figure 19.4. Observer Corps—a network of volunteer sky watchers. (Courtesy of Crown copyright.)

Figure 19.5. Observer Corps sky watchers—the eyes of the system.
(Courtesy of Kent Messenger Group Newspapers.)

One of Dowding's most significant contributions was the physical organization of RAF Fighter Command. He created a geographically distributed hierarchy of stations (group/sector) and airfields all networked (five years old) to the headquarters at Bentley Priory. Each sector had a main fighter air base with an operations room and maintenance and repair facilities and a number of other satellite fighter bases attached to it. He also insisted that concrete all-weather runways be built, and he got this wish granted with six airfields.

Despite the rise of fascism, the British were still striving for a peaceful solution. In February 1937, Dowding submitted a report to the government requesting the need for 45 operational fighter squadrons, 1,200 anti-aircraft guns, 5,000 searchlights, a functioning radar system, radio control of aircraft, and a massive expansion of the Observer Corps. The report was ignored.

The United Kingdom only began to rearm seriously after the Munich Crisis (1938) as the threat of war loomed. Even with the substantial increase in expenditure, the RAF lagged badly behind the Axis in the number of fighters. Production of fighters, in the hands of the Air Ministry, was woefully low and late.

By August 1939, Dowding had a fighter force of 34 squadrons when 52 squadrons were needed. Dowding was so concerned that he wrote to the Under Secretary of State for Air, Harold Balfour, and voiced his considerable misgivings as to Fighter Command's ability to defend the United Kingdom, conditional on supporting a defensive position in France.

Dowding's Losses

On May 10, 1940, the war in the West erupted. By May 13, the War Cabinet had agreed to send over an extra 32 Hurricanes and pilots to France, taken from different units across the United Kingdom. By the next day, the situation was even worse; the Axis broke through the French defensive lines. By nightfall, the French were asking for 10 more fighter squadrons. Dowding tried to stop additional fighters from going over to France because he thought the cause was lost in France and that sending more fighters would only deplete an already low home defence. Perturbed by mounting losses, he wrote a letter to the Air Ministry (16 May 1940), putting his won position on the line. This letter challenged Churchill over sending more fighter squadrons to France, after Churchill had personally promised these to the French Prime Minister Reynaud.

> I would remind the Air Council that the last estimate which they made as to the force necessary to defend this country was fifty-two squadrons, and my strength has now been reduced to the equivalent of thirty-six

squadrons. I must therefore request that as a
matter of paramount urgency the Air Ministry
will consider and decide what level of strength
is to be left to the Fighter Command for the
defence of this country, and will assure me
that when the level has been reached, not
one fighter will be sent across the Channel
however urgent and insistent the appeals for
help may be.

I believe that if an adequate fighter force
is kept in this country, if the Fleet remains
in being, and if Home Forces are suitably
organized to resist invasion, we should be
able to carry on the war single-handed for
some time, if not indefinitely. But, if the
Home Defence Force is drained away in
desperate attempts to remedy the situation
in France, defeat in France will involve the
final, complete and irremediable defeat of this
country.[2]

Dowding's was an uncomfortable truth that if France's
survival depended on the RAF, there would have to be a
sacrifice in the defence of the United Kingdom. Dowding
recognized when to cut losses. Churchill took the letter very
seriously, and this created a dilemma because of his promise.
In the end, squadrons were sent but operated in France during
the day and then returned at night to England. This action
further strained the Allied relationship. It did show Dowding's
incredible conviction to cause and his willingness to stand up
for it.

Dowding's Preparation for Battle

In May 1940, despite the lack of funding but because of his preparation and prudence, Dowding had made the right investments (radar, Observer Corps, distributed hierarchy of stations) to create all the basic components of a complex but sophisticated sense-and-respond system. This could not come soon enough because, despite his best efforts, RAF Fighter Command was facing a major challenge. With massive losses in the air battle over Flanders and France, he had to manage the remaining numbers of fighters very carefully in how he deployed them in the forthcoming battle.

By June 1940, an integrated air defence system was almost ready, with Bentley Priory, the operational headquarters, at the centre. Developed by Dowding, it had three unique mechanisms:

1. Sensing—an early-warning system consisting of three lines.

2. Decision making—a real-time environment with tools such as Executive Dashboards and real-time event models and processes for institutionalized decision making.

3. Responding—a system feeding information to a hierarchy of group/sector operations centres beneath it capable of responding to the threat.

Figure 19.6. Sense-and-respond concepts.

Sensing

Bentley Priory aggregated information from the following lines that provided early warning of incoming raids:

- The first line of the early-warning system was Bletchley Park, which passed top-secret Ultra information to Bentley Priory.[3] The Luftwaffe thought its encrypted communications were unbreakable. This top-grade intelligence would normally be of a strategic nature—the date and time of a raid, its size, the type of planes, and possibly the target. It would be passed to Bentley Priory in a very secure fashion, not directly to the operations room, but to handpicked individuals through a special liaison unit.

- The second line of the early warning system was made up of fifty radar stations. There were two types of complementary radar stations: long- and short-range. The former could pick up high-

169

flying enemy aircraft at 30,000 feet and up to 150 miles away, e.g., Paris, France. The latter had a shorter range but could pick up low-flying enemy aircraft. Both operated on pattern recognition and provided information on incoming raids. Radar information provided enemy position, direction, height, and estimated strength with a degree of accuracy. Radar crews operating both in the low and high-level stations aggregated this information. The aggregated information was phoned directly to a radar operation's command rooms or headquarters. This had a filter room where sightings and detection information could be aggregated, analyzed, and organized. The information was then passed by telephone on to the filter room at Bentley Priory for further processing.

Figure 19.7. Radar stations that made up the second line of the early warning system.

- The Observer Corps made up the third line of the early warning system. It consisted of civilian volunteers who, through binoculars, spotted incoming enemy aircraft. They identified and assessed the enemy aircraft strength from one thousand observation posts, based on the recognition of silhouettes and patterns. Radar was able to provide warning of enemy aircraft approaching the coast, but once they had crossed the coastline, the Observer Corps provided the only means of tracking them and could only track aircraft detected by the radar stations. Observer Corps information was aggregated by the Observer Corps headquarters, which in turn was passed by telephone on to the filter room at Bentley Priory for further processing.

Figure 19.8. Observer Corps headquarters (Courtesy of Kent Messenger Group Newspapers).

Together, the radar stations and Observer Corps covered nearly 90% of the United Kingdom's coastline.

Decision Making

The filter room at Bentley Priory headquarters was the communications hub that aggregated all this disparate information collected from the early-warning system. Occasionally, other sources, namely other operations centres and pilots, passed new information to Bentley Priory. All this information was integrated in real time and passed directly into the operations room, figure 19.9.

Figure 19.9. Bentley Priory Operational Centre plotting table gave a real-time view. (Courtesy of the Imperial War Museum, London.)

The Bentley Priory operations room, in reality, was a sophisticated real-time event model with an elegant user interface. Run by the Women of the Auxiliary Air Force (WAAFs), the purpose of the model was to map visually the skies above the United Kingdom. Through counters, the map table highlighted the location of both friendly and enemy aircraft on a scaled map of the United Kingdom. Through headsets, the WAAFs would receive information from the filter room. Enemy planes taking off in France were tracked and plotted onto this real-time model, reflecting every change. The counters on the glass-covered table were colour-coded:

- A red F on white background was for friendly aircraft,

- A black X on yellow meant unidentified, and

- A black H on yellow was for hostile (representing enemy formations) aircraft.

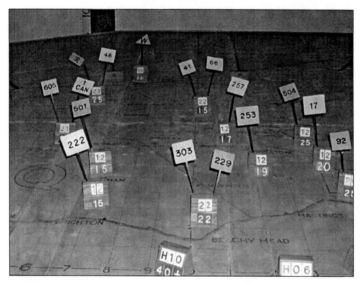

Figure 19.10. RAF Uxbridge Group 11 headquarters.

Every five minutes, the WAAFs changed the colour of all the enemy counters from yellow to red, and then to blue. These colours corresponded to the operations room's clock, which, in five-minute increments, was also colour coded (yellow, red, and blue). This provided a real-time snapshot of a raid in progress and its evolution.

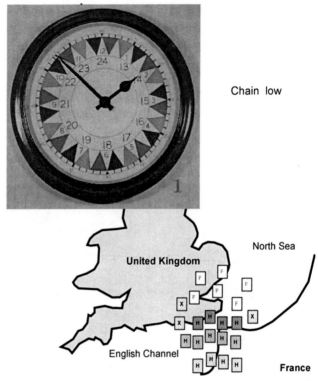

Figure 19.11. Map table with coloured counters representing aircraft coordinated with the clock.

When two stations gave the positions of the same aircraft, greater reliance was placed on the accuracy. A coloured arrow for each raid was changed as new reports were received. All the information on the table was no older than fifteen minutes, as the situation was continuously updated. As a result, the model provided a snapshot of real-time events, and this gave the decision-makers the information they needed to manage the movement of their fighters. They could position and group these fighters at the required operational heights to be most effective, which would prove to become a significant advantage.

Figure 19.12. Group Operations Centre. (Courtesy of Crown copyright.)

Responding

This information was then disseminated through the complete command structure, which divided the country into six groups (9, 10, 11, 12, 13, and 14), based geographically, see figure 19.13. Each group had a station and commanding air officer, and it was further divided into sectors (five to ten) with stations (headquarters) and surrounding, smaller fighter stations/ airfields.

175

Figure 19.13. RAF Fighter Command hierarchy supporting Bentley Priory. (Source: http://ibiblio.org/hyperwar/UN/UK/UK-RAF-I/maps/ UK-RAF-I-5.jpg.)

Within the individual group and sector operations centres were many of the characteristics of Bentley Priory, specifically with the event-tracking and decision-making environment. Bentley Priory at the centre saw the overall picture of events, whereas group levels saw only what pertained to them. The sector operations centres made up the front line, and they were expected to have the most activity (see figure 19.14).

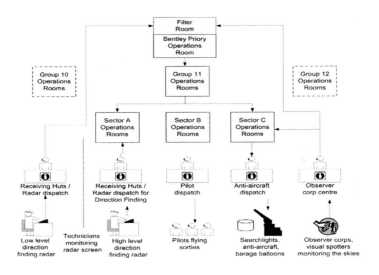

Figure 19.14. RAF Fighter Command hierarchy supporting Bentley Priory.

The group operations centres could then respond through a second user-interface model: the tote board. Named after the horseracing tracks' "Totalisator" board, it had dozens of electric lights that ran the full length of a wall. These indicated the status of squadrons—which squadrons in what sectors were in contact with the enemy or disengaging to refuel and rearm on the ground. It also indicated the operational state of readiness of squadrons held in reserve that were "available" in thirty minutes, at "readiness" in five minutes, or at "cockpit readiness" in two minutes to engage in immediate battle. This provided the decision-makers within the elevated gantry (see figure 19.12) a means to track the incoming raid and then respond through the tote model.

Figure 19.15. The tote board.

They could determine what resources were available and how they could be deployed. The sector level operations centres made the final decision that went out to the individual squadrons and pilots. The operations centres were also linked by telephone to following commands (see figure 19.14) that responded to incoming raids:

- The primary role of the anti-aircraft command, under the army, was to protect the aircraft manufacturing industry and support fighter command. It was divided nationally into seven divisions but linked to fighter command groups. Anti-aircraft fire was more effective in daylight than at night, as the incoming bomber streams were in closer formations. At night, the aircraft were very widely spaced with a 1:50 chance of a hit.

- Closely linked to the anti-aircraft command were the searchlight units, and they closely cooperated. Both had to be well aligned to the operational centres and aware of aircraft positions and movement in the skies to avoid firing on friendly fighters by mistake.

The barrage balloon command operated fifty-two squadrons across the United Kingdom, creating a barrage of large balloons that protected towns and cities as well as strategic targets such as industrial areas and ports. Strung by heavy cables, they protected everything at ground level from the threat of low-flying dive-bombers. Set at heights of up to 5,000 feet, they would force aircraft to fly high, limiting their accuracy, and bringing them within range of the anti-aircraft guns.

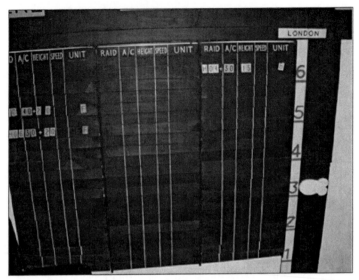

Figure 19.16. Tracking barrage balloons.

- Closely linked to Bentley Priory[4] were the operational training units that were responsible for pilot training. These units had to be aware of pilot losses as the number of available pilots was a continual problem for Dowding. Pilot training took three months and was limited to pilots under thirty. Dowding brought Allied pilots, as well as volunteers from the Commonwealth and countries under Axis occupation, into the RAF squadrons,

4. Air/sea rescue operations were directed to downed RAF pilots. Pilots were brought back to squadrons quickly and could be in the air on the same day.

5. Part of the Fighter Supply Chain and under the management of Beaverbrook at the Ministry of Aircraft Production (MAP), the Civilian Repair Operation (CRO) was an important recovery operation. MAP had a very tight relationship with

group operations who were in contact with their pilots and knew their positions in the battle, so they could plot the location of downed fighters very quickly.

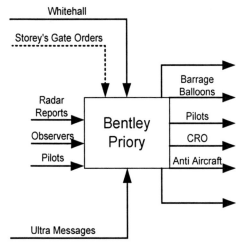

Figure 19.17. The inputs/outputs to Bentley Priory.

The whole operation, because of the flow of information, could readily track downed pilots and aircraft. The operation could also track and relate wastage by squadron and therefore direct the supply chain to re-supply where needed. Dowding, through Ultra, generally had a relatively good idea of where the targets were in advance. Dowding could use this information to give Beaverbrook a forecast to where supply likely would be needed.

Conclusion

In today's world, what can we take away from this lesson from history? Dowding made the right investment early on and thoroughly trained his minimal forces, but his preparation was ultimately put in jeopardy as the Allied forces collapsed in France. He conserved his resources against strong political pressure to disperse and misuse them and showed incredible conviction to cause.

Dowding's open and enquiring mind and his wish to become an engineer led to the building of the command structure for the new RAF Fighter Command. The completion of real-time event models and institutionalized decision making, known as the "Dowding System," influenced the course of the Battle of Britain. With a sophisticated early-warning system, it was the first time information had been used on such an industrial scale. The tracking of wastage and the ability to direct Beaverbrook's Civilian Repair Operation were important parts of the recovery operation and the Fighter Supply Chain. It was the first time information was used on such an industrial scale.

Key Lessons

In today's projects:

- Agile leaders are prepared to stand steadfast when the project is challenged or pulled off course.

- Agile leaders recognize that organizational agility also requires agility in organizational learning. It needs to be faster, more flexible, and more sensitive to the speed of individual experiential learning.

  And:

- Ensure modules work independently and have been tested before integrating into a solution.

- Ensure the integration effort is completed with clear objectives of the solution.

- Human Resource Management (PMBoK KA)—

- o Constantly look for opportunities for freeing up highly skilled top staff (pilots) from mundane activities.

- Cost Management (PMBoK KA)—

  - o With tight budgets, explore alternative approaches to get to the same goal. Pay attention to emerging technologies, their benefits, and impacts.

- Risk Management (PMBoK KA)—

  - o Ensure the risks in the use of emerging technologies are fully evaluated.

- Integration Management (PMBoK KA)—

  - o Establish dashboard(s) to provide metrics to help manage and control the sense-and-respond solution.

Educators

- Discuss Dowding's stand to Churchill in not sending further fighters to France.

- Discuss the use of Dowding's system in today's context and the manner in which real-time event models and early-warning systems can help improve and even institutionalize decision making.

CHAPTER TWENTY

Storey's Gate

This chapter looks at the fourth area of the overall project—*command and control of the whole system.* This was the final piece in the jigsaw, a command centre at the heart of the solution.

This chapter looks at how Churchill's need for an operational centre to support himself and tie into Beaverbrook and Dowding resulted in a facility known as Storey's Gate, or Churchill's Bunker, with an Executive Dashboard and decision-making environment.

In 1940, emerging technology had changed warfare to where agility was the new mode of operation in the military. New technology had mechanized warfare so armies could move rapidly. Armoured columns of concentrated strike power covered forty to fifty miles per day. Aircraft flying multiple sorties could strike four to five times a day. This agility or Blitzkrieg warfare came as a surprise to the Allies with a First World War mindset that still relied on fortified defences, immovable trenches, distributed artillery, and tanks.

The Battle of Flanders/France was a wake-up call for the British as agility was the new paradigm in modern warfare.

An agile war is dependent on making the best decisions quickly based on the best intelligence available, and this starts at a strategic level with the commander at the top passing strategic directives that are cascaded to operational leaders to make decisions and implement in the field. As a soldier, Churchill knew the importance of this. It was close to Downing Street and was designed to protect him and the War Cabinet from the expected air raids. Therefore, in May 1940, when he visited the newly completed underground facility Storeys Gate, he recognized the value of a secure and blast proof site as a new headquarters for the rest of the war and declared, "This is the room from which I will direct the war."[1]

The facility was to become the centre of the British War Machine and had to provide Churchill a conducive decision-making environment, so he could respond with agility. A principal facility of close collaboration made overriding decisions that affected the three other areas.

Work had originally started on Storey's Gate in June 1938 on adapting the storage areas ten feet below ground. The bombproof facility was designed to sleep and feed 270 people in 150 offices, rooms, and dormitories in a six-acre underground maze with more than a mile of corridors. At first glance, it was not a very appealing environment with rooms so gloomy that sun lamps were brought in to try to boost the vitamin D levels of workers. It became operational on 27 August 1939, just before Britain's declaration of war, but most planners saw it as no more than a temporary move.

Figure 20.1. Storey's Gate entrance to Churchill's Bunker.

The Cabinet War Room, the heart of Storey's Gate, was used for collaboration and real-time decision making at the most senior levels. Here, Churchill, embedded the military arms (chiefs of staff) into the War Cabinet to take part in all War Cabinet meetings, held daily to deal with all issues from military planning to food rationing. This is symbolized by the seating arrangement. In the First World War, he saw how the government was unable to unite the Army and Navy on the same page, and a lack of overall coordination existed. Churchill was determined to rectify this by building a close working relationship with the chiefs so that he could take competent actions based on reason and moral principles.

Establishing an Executive Dashboard

In today's world, an Executive Dashboard, based on business intelligence, provides a mechanism to monitor business activities and output and enables rapid decision making. The creation of an Executive Dashboard is driven by clear objectives or mission goals that help identify the critical success factors. With these established, meaningful real-time indicators can then be identified from readily available information.

In their simplest form, the processes required for establishing and running a successful executive dashboard include:

1. Collect information, establish Key Performance Indicators (KPIs), and set trigger thresholds.

2. Display the KPIs through an executive dashboard and trigger alerts.

3. Collaborate with decision-makers and experts to discuss alternatives and make decisions.

4. Take actions and mobilize forces.

Churchill's mission goals in May 1940 were very clear: he needed a snapshot of the war and a macro view of battle situations, and this had to be done in real time, or an Executive Dashboard in today's world. The critical success factors for this were related to the use, at a tactical level, of intelligence to preserve critical resources. Operational data that was readily available included production or manufacturing output, stock levels on fuel and ammunition, and resource losses (see figure 20.2).

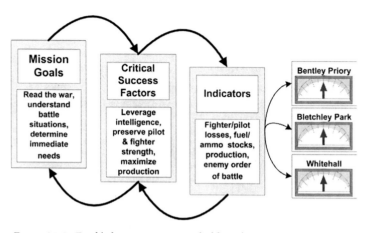

Figure 20.2. Establishing an executive dashboard.

In selecting KPIs, the MOst difficult task is to determine the suitability, usefulness, and validity of the data. For example, some financial indicators such as net profit and revenue reflect the past, and this information is not very useful for decision making. It only proves the existence of something, not what is currently happening.

Storey's Gate had to track the changing world and events for rapid complex decision making and for a real-time view at the highest (strategic) level. This required the creation of the equivalent of a "source-to-target data map" that defined how the source data, such as manufacturing and supply chain, found within the various environments were extracted, transformed, and loaded, and then converted to be used as indicators.

In today's world, as you go through this type of process, business rules are identified and documented, for example, how the data is produced, when, and in what format.

Storey's Gate needed meaningful real-time indicators. These were varied and included fighter indicators from Bentley Priory and the Air Ministry such as the availability of fighters and stockpiles of fuel to the supply chain for fighter production from Whitehall and the enemy order of battle indicators from Bletchley Park and other theatres of war (see figure 20.3 below).

SOURCE	LEAD INDICATORS (SUPPLIED DAILY)
Bentley Priory (and Air Ministry)	Fighter losses by squadron
	Number of sorties flown
	Pilots lost versus new pilots trained and available
	Enemy losses by aircraft type
	Fighter fuel and ammunition stocks available
	Civilian casualties
	Bombing damage to factories, loss in production
Whitehall (Ministry of Aircraft Production)	Fighter production numbers and delivery to airfields
	Raw materials/labour utilization (person hours in production)
	Key fighter-component production numbers and inventory
	CRO repair turnaround in timeframe
	Fighter engine imports from Canada
	Anti-aircraft production numbers
Bletchley Park	Indicators of enemy order of battle
	Enemy plans or intentions

Figure 20.3. Sources of operational data for Key Performance Indicators at Storey's Gate.

Some of the most critical information that was available to Storey's Gate was from Bletchley Park, and this required setting up secure direct lines and a special liaison unit.

Display KPIs Through an Executive Dashboard

Within Storey's Gate, a map room was created to display the indicators through real-time maps. The map room was effectively a real-time Executive Dashboard used for decision making. It had to present different types of indicators and content; the former was of particular importance. Indicators were carefully selected to provide early warning of a challenging situation or a specific event based on trigger thresholds, so timely, proactive decisions could be made, e.g., the availability of fighters and pilots was critical in battle situations as shown in figure 20.4. The pilot losses were by far the more critical.

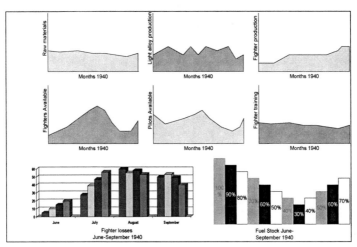

Figure 20.4. Executive Dashboard displaying KPIs.

The maps displaying indicators had to be incisive and intuitive, so visitors could rapidly absorb and grasp these to understand decisions and their repercussions. Figure 20.5 shows the broad spectrum of varied indicators from the supply chain and industrial production to stockpiles of fuel.

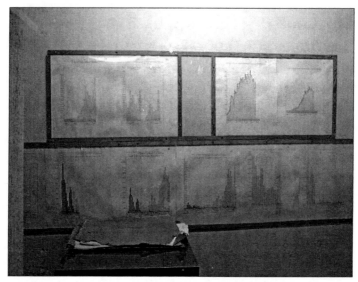

Figure 20.5. Actual Executive Dashboard at Storey's Gate.

The indicators had to be presented to the right person for decision making in a timely manner. Figure 20.6 shows another view that included indicators on enemy production.

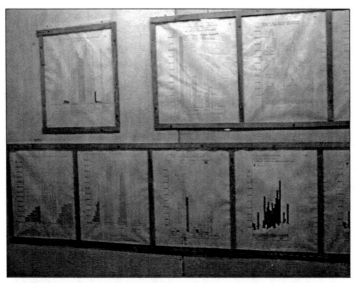

Figure 20.6: Second view of Executive Dashboard at Storey's Gate.

Officers running the map room plotted the information and indicators in real time (24 x 7) as shown in figure 20.7.

Figure 20.7. Plotting the Executive Dashboard with indicators.

Aside from indicators, other content/information that was also available from within Storey's Gate took many forms, including extracts from minutes and papers of top-level conferences, letters from the Foreign Office, and situation reports as shown in figure 20.8. This enhanced the primary information and helped fill in the blanks.

Figure 20.8. Content and information boards.

An Executive Dashboard drives qualitative improvements, reports performance against goals, establishes priorities, identifies ways to improve performance, highlights flaws in the operation, and ensures sustainability.

In the map room, he linked the military chain of hierarchy into this command centre. Decisions from the Cabinet War Rooms were transferred immediately to the underlying chains of command. Churchill incorporated the (armed forces) military structures into Storey's Gate and forced them to share some resources/expertise.

Figure 20.9: Map room's underlying Chains of Command.

With the map room, Churchill could readily follow events from all theatres of battle and have a big picture view, so he could respond accordingly. Churchill was so pleased with the map room that his architects created a travelling map room inside his personal railway carriage. As Churchill travelled across the United Kingdom visiting military installations, the travelling map room of lead indicators provided him a real-time pulse by which he could read the war, understand battle situations, and determine short-term needs. He could then communicate with the respective commanders and influence them in the control and performance of the supply chain and production. These lead indicators recognized events, such as changes in battlefronts that had a direct impact on the supply chain.

Figure 20.10. Churchill travelled across the United Kingdom visiting military installations. (Courtesy of Crown copyright.)

Conclusion

In today's world, what can we take away from this lesson from history? Churchill's use of dashboards, collaboration, and institutionalized decision making played a significant role in the course of the Battle of Britain. The map room supported the Cabinet War Room by tracking events, analysis, and real-time information. It cascaded actions to a vast network of linked commands. It processed real-time information for decision making and had a real-time view of all war theatres. Storey's Gate[2] became the centre of the overall system.

DEFINITION: "An adaptive enterprise (or adaptive organization) is an organization in which the goods or services demand and supply are matched and synchronized at all times. Such an organization optimizes the use of its resources (including its information technology resources), always using only those it needs and paying only for what it uses, yet ensuring that the supply is adequate to meet demand."[3]

Key Lessons

In today's projects:

- Agile leaders recognize the importance of real-time information for decision making.

- Agile leaders drive innovation and supervise its effectiveness.

- Agile leaders continuously identify, analyze, monitor, and respond to risk events.

- Agile leaders look for constant feedback and respond to it with change when it is required.

- Agile leaders take competent actions based on reason and moral principles.

    And:

- Risk Management (PMBoK KA)—

    ○ Focus on risk qualitative analysis to stay responsive.

- Integration Management (PMBoK KA)—

    ○ Establish dashboard(s) to provide metrics to help manage and control the sense-and-respond solution.

    ○ Ensure a high degree of testing occurs specifically with the integration aspects of a solution.

- Human Resource Management (PMBoK KA)—

    ○ Ensure a governance framework and organizational structure is in place prior to creating a physical organizational headquarters.

Educators

- Was it wise to locate the organizational headquarters in central London, a major target for attacks?

Agile Leadership and the Management of Change

CHAPTER TWENTY-ONE

Integration

This chapter examines how the basic components of the solution were brought together and integrated so that the flow of strategic information would allow the solution to operate as a complex sense-and-respond system or an Adaptive Enterprise.

The goal of the project was to integrate the four areas into a solution that could create an adequate defence to fend off an air invasion and prevent a sea invasion. The defence had to be sustained over a period. To understand the integration requirements of such a solution better, one approach is to lay it out as a simple supply chain, as shown in figure 21.1.

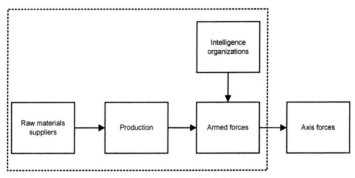

Figure 21.1. Solution outlined as a simple supply chain.

In simple terms, in order for the armed forces (RAF Fighter Command) to engage, there needed to be a steady flow of resources and information along the chain. The interactions within the supply chain were based on events, a stimulus (external, internal, or triggered by the passage of time) that prompted a reaction. Potential events impacting the supply chain are laid out in figure 21.2 below.

Event Description	Event Type
The demand for replacement equipment because of battle losses	External
Intelligence providing early warning of an imminent air attack	External
The loss of production by the bombing of industrial targets	External
The loss of convoy material and food supplies because of u-boat attacks	External
Inventory levels dropping below the reorder level	Internal
Armed forces withdrawing production of a certain type of obsolete equipment	Internal
Scientific breakthroughs in research and development, or new discoveries	Internal
Troops completing training and manouvers	Internal
Industrial production milestones, like resource mining or armaments output	Internal
Increase in supply and distribution of supplies like food	Internal
Overdue payments, month-end processing for production targets, stocktaking	Time

Figure 21.2. Events impacting the supply chain.

In such integration, events are relatively important as they determine how the supply chain should function. Figure 21.3 shows a more complex representation of Figure 21.2 with the interchange of information and intelligence and the supply-and-demand requirements along the chain including feedback loops and a decision-making body to provide guidance.

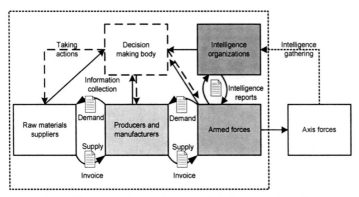

Figure 21.3. The supply chain solution with information interchanges.

The key problems In the integration of the four areas into this solution (or supply chain) lay in understanding how information was created and used by each organization, the interfaces and liaisons into the different chains of command, and the individual organizational structures. For example:

- What information would RAF Fighter Command require?

- How and what type of information would be exchanged by suppliers, producers, and manufacturers in the fighter supply chain?

- What were the principal methods of communication or channels?

- Would all the required information be available in a timely manner?

- What feedback information would be passed back and in what format?

These information exchanges set the constraints by which the solution would be bound.

Taking this a step further, figure 21.4 shows the solution as a supply-and-demand chain (see figure 21.4) with the four areas overlaying it.

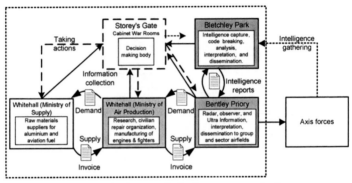

Figure 21.4. The supply chain with the four areas overlaid.

Each of the four areas in figure 21.4 was unique and had its own insights or individual views, and for this, it required different information, for example:

- Bentley Priory—Dowding and staff needed a view of enemy activity and forthcoming attacks, front line fighters available, fighter reserve, fighter wastage, and the production of fighters.

- Whitehall—at the Ministry of Air Production, Beaverbrook required horizontal views of the supply chain, fighter production, arms manufacturing, labour force, raw materials (Ministry of Supply), as well as the needs of RAF Fighter Command.

- Bletchley Park—Menzies and the intelligence chiefs and staff required a flow of Enigma information related to enemy activities and the ability to decode, interpret, and distribute it. They also acted like a feedback mechanism collecting information after actions were taken and determining the impact of these.

- Storey's Gate—Churchill and his staff, cabinet ministers, and chiefs of staff needed to be in touch with all the areas across the solution. This was a principal community that made the overriding decisions that affected the other areas.

The solution (or system) had to adapt to changing conditions and regulate itself. This required a high level of integration, the rapid interchange of information, and unifying the four areas into a "big picture" that operated as a single adaptive or sense-and-respond solution: "An adaptive system is a system that is able to adapt its behaviour according to changes in its environment or in parts of the system itself. A human being, for instance, is certainly an adaptive system; so are organizations and families. Some manmade systems can be made adaptive as well; for instance, control systems utilize feedback loops in order to sense conditions in their environment and adapt accordingly. Robots incorporate many of these control systems. Neural networks are a common type of algorithmic implementation of adaptive systems." [1]

In retrospect, the whole system was adaptive. The four areas had to exchange information vital to the overall operation of the solution; without it, the solution could not respond to incoming threats. For example, through the Battle of Britain, a daily interchange was required between Beaverbrook and Dowding to report the daily fighter losses or wastage. In another example, Bletchley Park had to provide daily Ultra decrypts to Churchill personally at Storey's Gate. Figure 21.5

shows the basic information interchange between the four areas.

Destination / Source	Bentley Priory	Bletchley Park	Whitehall (MAP)	Storey's Gate
Bentley Priory	Management decision making	Requests for intelligence	Downed fighter locations, CRO	Fighter/pilot loss reports
Bletchley Park	Order of battle report	Management decision making	Enemy supply chain, resources	Ultra decrypts, reports
Whitehall (MAP)	Fighter production report	Orders, requests	Management decision making	Supply chain indicators
Storey's Gate	Orders, requests	Orders, requests	Orders, requests	Executive decision making

Figure 21.5. The source and destination for information interchange.

All along the supply chain, the solution would have to handle large volumes of disparate data from multiple sources and convert it into useful intelligence in a timely manner. This required a high degree of organization and a data governance framework.

The information would be available from multiple sources and in different formats, such as paper, image, electronic, and voice. The main interfaces or channels for exchanging information were through the telephone or teleprinter, as shown in figure 21.6. The same channel could not always be used in both directions because of the security of certain information.

Source \ Destination	Bentley Priory	Bletchley Park	Whitehall (MAP)	Storey's Gate
Bentley Priory	Face to face, Telephone	None	Telephone	Telephone
Bletchley Park	SLU	Face to face	Via Storey's Gate	SLU
Whitehall (MAP)	Telephone, Teleprinters	None	Face to face, Telephone	Telephone
Storey's Gate	Telephone, Teleprinters	Face to face	Telephone, Teleprinters	Face to face

Figure 21.6. The interfaces or channels for information exchange.

Some of the integration within the solution would be particularly challenging because of these security implications. For example, information provided by Bletchley Park would be very problematic, and great caution had to be taken in handling Ultra so that it was not disseminated through an insecure interface into an organizational hierarchy prone to security breaches.

The security of information flow to individuals was a major challenge because Ultra had to be kept secret at all times and all costs. After all, any giveaway to the enemy that the codes had been broken would be very acute because of security implications. The codes would be changed or not used at all.

As a solution, Bletchley Park created special liaison units (SLUs) under the auspices of RAF Captain Fred Winterbotham for the sole task of security and distribution of information, so Churchill could be briefed daily. These were to be connected to Storey's Gate and Bentley Priory, and information from a top-secret source would be distributed to the Director of Intelligence located there, as shown in the figure below. The dissemination of information performed by the SLUs was done through different secure channels, such as isolated teleprinters, courier bags, and scrambler phones.

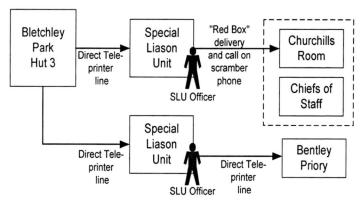

Figure 21.7. The dissemination of information through SLUs.

Eventually, following Churchill's concerns about security leaks, the list of recipients for Ultra was strictly limited to nine people. SLUs were located at Bletchley Park and then later overseas in Gibraltar, Malta, Cyprus, and Egypt to be closer to the front lines.

In a complex adaptive enterprise, the areas requiring integration are typically at different levels of development and maturity. The approach to build, integrate, and test needs to be driven by a release strategy that is prioritized by the criticality of events (see figure 21.2). With Churchill's solution, there was little difference in approach. For example, an imminent enemy raid on RAF airfields (high) was by far more critical than an enemy raid on towns or cities (low); as callous as it may seem, knocking out the primary defence mechanism would be more costly in casualties in the longer run.

Figure 21.8 outlines sample events, the area(s)/ sub-areas involved in identifying or sensing these, the area(s) involved in responding to the events and the types of actions taken.

#	Event Description	Priority of Event	Area(s) / Sub-areas Responsible for Sensing Event	Area(s) Responsible for Responding to Events	Action and Response Required
1	Imminent enemy raid on RAF airfields	H	Radar, observers, Ultra	Bentley Priory, Storey's Gate, Whitehall	Deploy fighters
2	Imminent enemy raid on industrial targets	M	Radar, observers, Ultra	Bentley Priory, Storey's Gate, Whitehall	Deploy fighters and anti-aircraft
3	Imminent enemy raid on towns and cities	L	Ultra, radar, observers	Bentley Priory, Storey's Gate, Whitehall	Deploy fighters and anti-aircraft
4	Low fuel reserves	H	Supply chain, Whitehall	Storey's Gate, Whitehall	Increase convoy fuel shipments
5	Low ammunition reserves	H	Supply chain, Whitehall	Storey's Gate, Whitehall	Redeploy resources
6	Low food stocks	L	Supply chain, Whitehall	Storey's Gate, Whitehall	Negotiate with allies
7	Low fighter engine parts	M	Supply chain, Whitehall	Storey's Gate, Whitehall	Negotiate with allies
8	Ultra compromised	H	Enemy actions raise suspicions at Bletchley Park	Storey's Gate, Bletchley Park	Determine breach, consider options
9	North Atlantic convoy losses	L	Supply chain, Whitehall	Storey's Gate, Whitehall	Redeploy resources, protection
10	RAF raids to disrupt invasion assembly areas	M	Storey's Gate, military	Storey's Gate, Bletchley Park	Redeploy resources

Figure 21.8. Areas responsible for sensing and responding to events.

Each event had to be carefully considered to determine how it would be sensed and the area(s)/sub-areas targeted to respond to it, as there could be several. From this, the "if-then" conditional logic could be determined to create the action and response to the event based on the overall complexity. In addition, thought had to be given in how this would be tested.

Churchill's architects, under tremendous time pressure, had to look at what could be delivered in a very short timeframe, what needed completion, and what could be put off. The priority of completion and deployment related to completing the sense-and-respond solution at Bentley Priory and Bletchley Park, so high-priority events could be responded to, e.g., events 1, 4, 5, and 8 from figure 21.8. Bentley Priory was a higher priority than Whitehall, so resources were prioritized, and there was no clash over these.

Conclusions

The solution integrated Churchill's Cabinet War Rooms with "Dowding's System," Beaverbrook's "Supply Chain," and Bletchley Park's "Ultra." These were all at different levels of development and maturity. The entire complex system (adaptive enterprise) had to operate as a single integrated system, sensing events and responding to these. It truly was the centre of the British War Machine.

Key Lessons

In today's projects:

- Agile leaders recognize that an agile organization requires well-integrated systems for passing information.

And:

- Risk Management (PMBoK KA)—

○ In gathering requirements, the focus is not just on the functional, but also the non-functional requirements. Getting the latter wrong is a far more risky and costly proposition to the project

- Time Management (PMBoK KA)—

  ○ In a complex integration project schedule, the most difficult integration elements first.

Educators

In today's world, integration points drive integration projects. Discuss the complexity of the overall solution.

CHAPTER TWENTY-TWO

Approach to Testing the Solution

This chapter examines how the solution was tested to the breaking point and made operational in readiness for the forthcoming air battle.

Dowding's system could give RAF Fighter Command a distinct advantage in "vectoring" fighters to points in the sky where they could ambush enemy aircraft. This would increase the ability to concentrate fighters quickly, and pilots would not have to waste time and fuel searching large expanses of sky looking for the enemy. Simple in concept, the challenge lay in the ability to deploy the solution and to scale it up and ensure it worked according to design.

The overall approach needed to complete a comprehensive strategy for testing the effectiveness of the solution in terms of its early-warning components and its ability to scramble fighters to meet raids. The approach started small (unit test) by testing the reaction to single-fighter raids. It then scaled up to test reactions to multiple raids (integrated test) and those by large bomber formations (system test).

The principal objective of the testing was to test the detection of enemy planes and then the scrambling of fighters. To achieve this, enemy formations had to be detected well in advance, as fighters needed at least fifteen minutes of early warning to scramble and climb to a height of 20,000 feet. The pilots had a margin of safety of a few minutes in racing into their positions.

Testing was critical for Bentley Priory, at the heart of the system, particularly testing the overall sense and response times, and this could only be tested dynamically. At Bentley Priory, the environment was set up for testing the early-warning system and fighter scrambles by using individual radar stations and observer posts as part of the test environment. Friendly aircraft from the northern groups simulated enemy raids by flying over the southern coast to test the effectiveness of the early-warning system as realistically as possible. Even the testers were unaware that the aircraft were friendly.

For weeks, the entire early-warning system, interlinking all the various components and the four integrated areas, was tested incessantly as it was pushed to the breaking point, with squadrons of British aircraft simulating incoming enemy formations. The iterative approach to testing allowed precious seconds to be shaved off the overall fighter response times as the early-warning system was honed to a peak of efficiency for scrambling fighters. As this testing evolved, the RAF was able to perfect a formula to intercept enemy raids.

As testing completed, the solution was loaded incrementally into production. The initial release focused on

- The integration of Bentley Priory to the Group 11 operations centres and its network of radar, pilots, and observers who were likely to see 90% of all action. The groups furthest from the fighting (10 and 12) were deployed last.

- It was important to keep a broad focus and holistic view of all aspects of the solution, so information from supply-chain indicators was made available to Whitehall, and as a result, to Storey's Gate. For Whitehall, the urgency was getting fighter production metrics to Storey's Gate.

- At Bletchley Park, all manual procedures were completed and incrementally loaded.

Once in production, the final testing put each of the increments through what we call acceptance and operability testing. It also refined service-level objectives (SLOs) and agreements.

- The acceptance testing required satisfying a number of executive sponsors/players, notably Churchill, Beaverbrook, and Dowding who were principal "users" of the first releases. The testing was particularly important for these users who were looking for how well they were equipped for decision making with the information provided and the functionality of the solution.

- At Bentley Priory, the Women's Auxiliary Air Force (WAAFs) completed the operability tests using the operations centre's map table. Bentley Priory's primary goal was to meet an imminent enemy raid on target with either fighters or anti-aircraft. Fighters had to be vectored to the right place, at the right time, and airborne at 20,000 feet in formation to face the imminent raid. Timing was critical. Any delays meant pilots would lose crucial height advantage, so they had to be available on standby at any point in daylight hours.

- To achieve SLOs meant fighters had to be scrambled and positioned in three minutes. This was based on the short channel-crossing time for enemy aircraft flying at 300 mph (or 5 miles per minute) across the 40 miles to the English coast in eight minutes, sector airfields in twelve minutes, and London in twenty minutes.

• To refine the SLOs meant the service-delivery chain of processes had to be examined to determine what was required in each process to achieve the overall goal of a three-minute fighter scramble time, for example, fighters depended on a sector operations centre passing an imminent raid warning in under a minute. Likewise, group operations centres had to pass their warnings in under a minute. Hence, the chain in figure 22.1 emerged below.

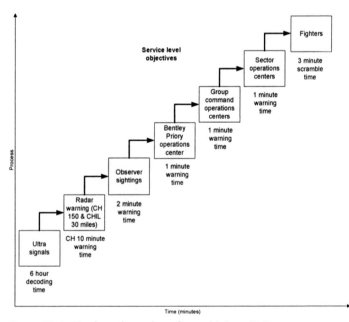

Figure 22.1. The dependency chain for establishing SLOs.

The dependency chain for SLOs provided a starting framework for establishing measurable goals, in this case, for scrambling fighters. Each process in the service-delivery chain was examined to determine what it had to achieve to meet the overall goal of a three-minute fighter scramble.

Dowding's team spent many weeks testing and refining the fighter-scramble SLAs, reducing precious seconds across the whole service-delivery chain. By tracking this, Dowding's team could readily measure the battle success rate of early airborne fighters and correlate it to scramble times. In addition, this overall early-warning system preserved precious fuel stocks by maximizing fighter time on the ground and by targeting them accurately at enemy planes.

A holistic view of the solution and the eventual integration through release 2 is shown in figure 22.2 below. Storey's Gate was the overall command centre for the whole operation. Although the other areas operated autonomously, it was the master of masters, Bentley Priory and the fighter supply chain, managing the big picture and tightly integrated to Bletchley Park. Based on accurate and timely information and intelligence, Churchill and his organization would be better able to understand what was going on in the broader picture of the war. They followed the air battle, closely monitored the supply chain, and kept track of events from other battlefronts. They would be better able to leverage all the resources at their disposal, select the best tactics and determine the most promising strategies and projects. Storey's Gate would become the principal facility for conducting the war.

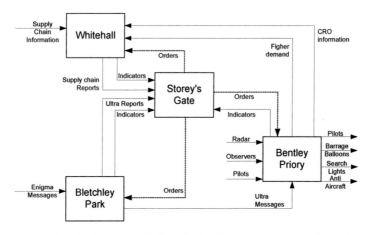

Figure 22.2. Holistic view of Churchill's solution (four integrated areas).

Conclusion

In summary, Churchill's solution was the equivalent to a modern adaptive enterprise in which an organization can act with agility and capitalize on change. The solution simplified complex situations and provided insights that improved decision making in real time. This required synchronization between the business and the underlying infrastructure (today's IT).

Key Lessons

In today's projects:

- Agile leaders recognize that adequate time needs to be allocated to testing an adaptive enterprise at different levels (acceptance and operational tests) to lessen the risk.

- Agile leaders recognize that testing of an adaptive enterprise is complex.

- Agile leaders simplify complex situations (through tools) and use sound judgments to make good decisions at the right time.

And:

- Risk Management (PMBoK KA)—

  o In a complex integration project, ensure adequate time is allocated to testing the functional and non-functional requirements of the solution. Getting the latter wrong is a far more risky and costly proposition to the project.

Educators

- From a project perspective, was enough time spent in testing such an important solution?

CHAPTER TWENTY-THREE

Historical Events of June and July 1940

The previous four chapters looked at how Churchill's organization prepared itself for the air battle to meet his short-term objectives of staving off the invasion and how it put together a solution. This chapter switches gears and enters the final phase of the book that examines the historical sequence of events between June and October 1940. This analysis will reflect on the effectiveness of Churchill's solution and its utilization.

One of the most difficult questions to answer with any project is did it meet the requirements and reach its goals? Did the output (solution) achieve what it was designed to do? Did it assist in a critical situation and help the organization react to it?

In early June 1940, most of the news for Churchill was bad. It indicated an imminent invasion and a poor state of readiness in the British defences. The first phase of the battle opened up while the Battle of France still raged with the Luftwaffe making small active operations against the United Kingdom to reconnoitre airfields, harass the civilian population, and disrupt industry. Here is a daily breakdown of key responses through June:

- 1st—Fighter command learned of 509 fighters lost in Norway and France. An adequate defence needed 52 squadrons, but only 28 were available. Beaverbrook stepped up production (chapter 18).

- 4th—Ultra indicated massive troop movements and invasion preparation on the French coast. Therefore, the War Cabinet targeted enemy ports and the invasion barges for RAF Bomber Command as "top priority." A significant first use of Ultra (chapter 19) highlighted its enormous potential for Churchill. The Luftwaffe operated with well-dispersed aircraft from over 400 airfields and so was more difficult to target. On the same day, Churchill learned the true cost of the Dunkirk evacuation. The British army had only 200 heavy/medium tanks and 300 light tanks, so he ordered production to be stepped up.

Figure 23.1: Invasion barges off the French coast became targets. (Courtesy of Crown copyright.)

- 5th—The War Cabinet (chapter 18), worried about labour unrest impacting essential war production, banned strike action for workers.

- 6th—Storey's Gate indicators (chapter 21) still showed a shortfall in military production. Vital resources were still being diverted. Therefore, the production of hundreds of household goods was banned.

- 17th—The tight supply of machine tools and their high cost in U.S. dollars impacts fighter production. All production departments agreed that future orders would be brought under the single auspices of the British Purchasing Commission.

- 18th—General de Gaulle fled to London and rallied the Free French resistance. He issued a radio appeal for the French nation to resist and to continue the struggle.

- 20th—The War Cabinet learned that the French, under Marshal Petain, signed an armistice with Germany. An invasion alert was put out to military forces in the United Kingdom.

- 23rd—Hitler made a brief tour of occupied Paris.

- 25th—Increased income taxes were introduced in the U.S. to pay for Roosevelt's armament expenditures and bring in an additional 2.2 million taxpayers.

- 30th—Incredibly, Beaverbrook (chapters 17/18) managed to raise monthly fighter production from 292 to 446. Much of this can be attributed to introduction of best practices, sheer force of will with the removal of production bottlenecks and obstacles, and the reallocation of vital resources.

The above decisions and actions highlight the increased awareness in the War Cabinet of what was happening in the economy at a macro level. All stops were pulled out to accelerate fighter production to reach truly impressive numbers by the end of the month.

In July 1940, the news became worse for Churchill and indicated the start of the second phase of the air battle when Luftwaffe bombers attacked coastal convoys, ports on the south coast to assess the air defences, and the agility of the RAF response. Churchill recognized the potential of the solution and skillfully bought time to complete it. Here is a daily breakdown of key responses through July:

- 1st—Churchill was so pleased with the map room that his architects created a "travelling" map room (chapter 21) inside his personal railway carriage. As he travelled across the United Kingdom visiting military installations, it provided him all the lead indicators with which to read the war, understand battle situations, and determine short-term needs.

- 2nd— Churchill learned what troops and guns were available in coastal areas, grilled field commanders on the state of readiness, and increased pressure on them.

- 3rd—French Admiral Gensoul was offered choices to ensure his fleet stayed out of Axis hands. All were turned down, and the Royal Navy opened fire on the anchored ships. One blew up and the other three ships were badly damaged. For the British, "a hateful decision but no act more necessary…"[1] against their former French allies showed Churchill's ruthless determination to cause, and it impressed Roosevelt that Churchill was a man of action and not bluster.

- 4th—Churchill learned through Ultra (chapter 19) that Italian troops had entered Sudan, and he was faced with a second battlefront and a difficult decision to direct resources there.

- 10th—Beaverbrook learned of shortages in essential materials for fighter production (chapter 17). He appealed for aluminium goods, pots, and pans. The collection raised public morale, as they believed that "they were doing their bit."

- 14th—Based on low morale indicators (chapter 13), Churchill was motivated to broadcast a rousing speech. Not since Elizabeth I, had anyone spoken of the English like this, and the nation's morale was elevated.

- 15th—Ultra messages decoded by Bletchley Park (chapter 17) revealed enemy intent and strength of 1,700 bombers and 1,100 fighters against 600 British fighters. On the same day, Dowding was under pressure to change tactics and respond en masse. He resisted and relied on his early-warning system with Churchill's full support.

- 16th—Ultra (chapter 17) revealed the scale of "Operation Sea Lion," but with Ultra established, up to two hundred decoded messages a day are passed to Bentley Priory.[2]

- 19th—Churchill learned of Hitler's peace offers with which Germany would have control of Europe, and in return, Britain's empire would be safe. Churchill eventually rejected the terms but only after he bought precious time to prepare further for battle.

- 20th—Churchill saw conflicting priorities impacting essential war production (chapter 21). The buying and selling of new cars was banned.

- 23rd—Churchill learned that the Soviet Union had occupied Lithuania, Latvia, and Estonia. There was no possibility of an alliance as long as the Soviets/Nazis pact held.

Figure 23.2. July 24—Taken from a Luftwaffe bomber, an RAF fighter crossing its path. (Courtesy of Crown copyright.)

- 28th—Fighting intensified in the Channel as the Luftwaffe attacked convoys with the aim of weakening the Royal Navy, damaging United Kingdom trade, and wearing down fighter forces. The Royal Navy withdrew its destroyers from Dover to safer harbours.

- 31st—Beaverbrook learned of spare aircraft part storage controlled by the Air Ministry (chapter 17). He forcibly gained control and moved the parts into production to eliminate the inventory.

Overall, there was a frantic preparation to complete early releases of the solution. Churchill had to convince the nation to fight on and initiated his communication plan.

Conclusion

In this early period, the solution was providing the key players (Churchill, Beaverbrook, and Dowding) with critical information to improve their decision making and better meet objectives. The focus was principally on Beaverbrook's organization, and in a short time, the progress was remarkable when measured just in production numbers. However, Beaverbrook was aware that workers in the main aircraft fighter factories were working long shifts of twelve to fourteen hours per day, and this rate could not be kept up over several months.

By cutting through government red tape and using Beaverbrook's initiatives, the Ministry increased production by 250% in what was once a faltering industry. By the end of July, despite attacks of British aircraft facilities, fighter production continued to hit an astounding figure of 496 Spitfires and Hurricanes per month (see figure 3). This was considerably more than the German production at the time.

Key Lessons

In today's projects:

- Agile leaders are able to switch focus rapidly when required.

- Agile leaders depend on an agile organization that is relatively "flat" (two to three hierarchical levels) with agile team (sub) leaders leading departments.

  And:

- Scope Management (PMBoK KA)—

  o Roll out piecemeal and hit the neediest areas. Review the initial cost/benefit analysis to determine how successful (or not) the solution on rollout is and what needs to be adjusted.

- Risk Management (PMBoK KA)—

  o Review the risks in implementation.

- Integration Management (PMBoK KA)—

  o Beaverbrook achieved astounding results, and he was assisted by good metrics in his decision making.

Educators

- From a project perspective, was enough time spent in testing such an important solution?

CHAPTER TWENTY-FOUR

Historical Events of August 1940

This chapter examines August 1940 for the utilization and the effectiveness of Churchill's solution. It tries to answer the most difficult question of any project, namely, did it meet the requirements and reach its goals? Did the output (solution) achieve what it was designed to do? Did it assist in a critical situation and help the organization react to it?

The third phase of the battle started in August as the attacks on shipping continued, but bombing raids started to concentrate on RAF airfields.

Figure 24.1. Channel action (Courtesy of Crown copyright.)

The Luftwaffe struck its first real blow against Fighter Command's ground organization. Here is a daily breakdown of key responses through August:

- 1st—Hitler's order No. 17 instructed the Luftwaffe to begin air attacks on Britain as preparation for invasion. Churchill and Dowding learned of the order and prepared for the ensuing air battle.

- 8th—Heavy fights broke out over the Channel with 150 aircraft involved. The Luftwaffe lost 31 aircraft, the RAF 19. Dowding monitored the air battle closely, and Beaverbrook monitored the losses, so he could adjust production (Chapter 17).

- 9th—Bletchley Park (Chapter 19) passed repeated warning messages that indicated a massive forthcoming attack on "Eagle Day." Intelligence indicated the enemy believed the RAF could be defeated in four days. Dowding learned that Göring was looking for an all-out assault and the destruction of as many fighters in large set battles.

- 10th—Bentley Priory learned of a shortfall in pilot replacement numbers. The operation-training period for qualified pilots was cut from six months to two weeks.

- 12th—Bentley Priory learned of attacks on its airfields and coastal radar stations. The attack in the Southeast was met. Surprisingly, it did not continue on subsequent days. The Luftwaffe did not recognize the importance of radar towers (chapter 20), which were very difficult to knock out from the air. On the same day, worried about a food crisis, the government made the wasting of food illegal.

- 13th—Eagle Day, and enemy aircraft activity over the United Kingdom was on a scale far in excess of anything before. Storey's Gate learned of enemy night raids on two fighter factories. The attack indicated night bombers carried a sophisticated guidance system. Beaverbrook was on high alert.

- 14th—Churchill received a message from Roosevelt offering a trade of destroyers/planes for U.S. military bases on British soil (figure 24.2). The offer was immediately accepted and seen as a step towards Churchill's longer-term strategy.

Figure 24.2. A trade of destroyers/planes for U.S. military bases on British soil. (Courtesy of Illustrated London News.)

- 15th—Apprised by Ultra, radar, and Observer Corps, Dowding was ready for battle. Bentley Priory carefully preserved its resources and avoided stretching these to the utmost. Dowding sought to prevent all-out fighter battle. A day of intense attacks, the Luftwaffe launched 1,790 sorties and lost 75 planes to the RAF's 34.

- 16th—Bentley Priory recognized attacks were only against its airfields and fighters within Group 11 and the vital sector stations that controlled its squadrons. Targets spared included the vital radar stations. Bentley Priory learned of heavy fighter losses, so the defensive strategy was adjusted accordingly so that faster Spitfire fighters were sent in first while the slower Hurricanes were pitted against bombers.

- 16th—RAF Fighter Command had now fallen 209 pilots below "minimum acceptable strength." Life expectancy of a British fighter pilot was less than 87 flying hours. Exhaustion took such a heavy toll on the survivors that many of them routinely fell asleep as they taxied their aircraft to a stop. It was common for ground crews to remove a sleeping pilot from his plane when he returned from combat.[1]

- 18th—Dowding learned that fighter command was under tremendous pressure. A fourth day of raids continued to devastate sector stations around London.

- 19th—Bentley Priory got a short respite, as the Luftwaffe paused. Luftwaffe losses were 236 against 213 RAF (in ten days). Dowding knew RAF losses were unsustainable. Bentley Priory learned from Whitehall of fighter production-rate shortfall. Beaverbrook appealed to the civilian repair organization (CRO) to increase their shifts to get aircraft back in the air (Chapter 18). On the same day, all of the United Kingdom was declared a defence area.

- 20th—Churchill broadcasted his recognition of pilots' speech from Storey's Gate, "Never in the field of human conflict was so much owed by so many to so few."[2] An important part of his communication plan (Chapter 13), this broadcast rallied morale but also reached the U.S. audience and Roosevelt simultaneously.

- 21st—Nationalist forces of Poland, Norway, Belgium, Holland, France, and Czechoslovakia could train in the United Kingdom under their own flags.

- 22nd—Storey's Gate learned of the worsening situation in the Middle East. Churchill took a massive gamble and dispatched a convoy with 150 tanks. The War Cabinet learned that financial reserves would be exhausted in four months. Beaverbrook urged continued purchase of American materials to tie the U.S. closer to Britain's cause, part of Churchill's longer-term strategy (Chapter 9).

Figure 24.3. August 22. (Courtesy of Kent Messenger Group Newspapers.)

- 24th—Dowding learned of further attacks on the RAF resulting in the very bad damage of main sector airfields. At this point, *the RAF was twenty-four hours from defeat if attacks were sustained* because the losses were running at a fatal rate. Whitehall informed Storey's Gate of further raids on aircraft factories in which Spitfire and Hurricane production was affected. Churchill learned of an attack on the suburbs of London. Twelve German bombers, unable to locate their targets during an unusual night attack, scattered their bombs aimlessly on South London despite strict orders from Hitler forbidding attacks on civilian targets, especially the city of London. Nine civilians were killed.

- 25th—The War Cabinet ordered a reprisal raid on Berlin. Although the British raid was small, the German population was shocked. Hitler and Göring were dismayed, ordered massive retaliation, and changed the targets to the city of London.

- 30th—Bentley Priory was aware of a huge fighter attack. Dowding ordered RAF fighters to disengage where possible against such odds. Bletchley Park decoded a message stating that Hitler would determine the invasion date on September 10, potentially September 20. Bentley Priory was aware that the RAF was at its breaking point. RAF pilots flew a total of a thousand sorties in a single day; some pilots flew four sorties without rest. The Luftwaffe had lost 600 aircraft versus the RAF's 260, but the cost was heavy for RAF in terms of experienced pilots.

By the end of August, with good visibility across the supply chain, Beaverbrook managed to align his fighter supply chain closely to RAF Fighter Command demand. Every evening throughout the Battle of Britain, he was in contact with its leader Dowding who reported his daily fighter losses. Beaverbrook was able to introduce the concepts of just-in-time manufacturing and was able to build to demand and deliver specifically to depleted squadrons on a daily basis. By the end of August, fighter production continued to hit an astounding number of 476 per month.

Conclusion

Did Churchill's solution meet the requirements and reach its goals? In this middle period, the solution was to provide the key players (Churchill, Beaverbrook, and Dowding) with critical information to improve their decision making and better meet objectives. The answer is not conclusive.

Did the output achieve what it was designed to do? The focus was principally on Dowding's organization, and it helped by tracking the battle (next chapter) and providing accurate metrics. Dowding could readily adjust his tactics and rode out what the enemy perceived to be a short four-day battle.

Did it assist in a critical situation and help the organization react to it? In this period, *Churchill's decisions were also truly monumental* by first, dispatching two armoured divisions to the Middle East and secondly, by retaliating with bombers against Berlin. The latter changed the course of the air battle.

Key Lessons

In today's projects:

- Agile leaders such as Dowding were able to adjust tactics rapidly at short notice.

- Agile leaders such as Beaverbrook were able to remove bottlenecks from the supply chain.

  And:

- Scope Management (PMBoK KA)—

  o Roll out piecemeal, and hit the neediest areas. Review the initial cost/benefit analysis to determine how successful (or not) the solution on rollout is and what needs to be adjusted.

  o Risk Management (PMBoK KA)—

  o Review the risks in implementation.

- Integration Management (PMBoK KA)—

  o Beaverbrook achieved astounding results, and he was assisted by good metrics in his decision making.

Educators

- How sound were Churchill's decisions to dispatch two armoured divisions to the Middle East?

CHAPTER TWENTY-FIVE

Historical Events of September 1940

This chapter examines September 1940 for the utilization and the effectiveness of Churchill's solution. Again, it tries to answer the most difficult question of any project, namely, did it meet the requirements and reach its goals? Did the output (solution) achieve what it was designed to do? Did it assist in a critical situation and help the organization react to it?

The fourth phase of the battle started in September with "the Blitz" when the city of London was heavily bombed, as Hitler and Luftwaffe chief Hermann Göring hoped to destroy the morale of the British people in retaliation for the RAF bombing raids on Berlin (August 24–29).

For the German high command, London became an attractive target. In 750 square miles, there was a concentration of about 9,000,000 people, or one-fifth of the population of the United Kingdom. It became the target of massed assault by the enemy's bombers and the theory of a knockout blow that the enemy would aim at the country's nerve centre. This was influenced by the relatively quick capitulations of Poland and the Netherlands following attacks on civilian populations in the capitals.

The Luftwaffe struck against London and the cities to destroy civilian morale. Here is a daily breakdown of key responses through September:

- 1st—The War Cabinet learned of attacks on the populations and big cities. Hitler mistakenly believed his fighters had mastery of the skies.

- 5th—Bentley Priory realized the switch in enemy tactics to London was ongoing. The news was significant, as it allowed Dowding to rebuild Group 11 squadrons.

- 6th—The War Cabinet learned RAF losses were creeping up to Luftwaffe levels. The RAF lost 466 fighters and received 269 new ones; 103 pilots were killed and 128 wounded. RAF Fighter Command was close to defeat.

- 7th—Bletchley Park failed to warn Dowding of a massive 900-aircraft attack. Too few pilots were in position to defend London adequately, and London sustained major damage. Storey's Gate issued an alert: "invasion imminent and probable in 12 hours."[1] Churchill ordered Bomber Command to attack the channel ports crammed with 1,000 barges. Meanwhile Göring travelled to French ports to see off 300 German bombers escorted by 600 fighters to attack London docks. London was the heart of the largest trading empire and handled a phenomenal amount of trade through its docks. At night, 250 bombers used blazing fires to guide attacks, resulting in severe damage.

Figure 25.1: Blitz on London docks. (Courtesy of Crown copyright.)

- 8th—Churchill broadcasted his defiance to bombing in a speech from Storey's Gate. "…A people who will not flinch of the struggle—hard and protracted though it will be."[2]

- 9th—Dowding learned of huge incoming raids and switched tactics and operated squadron pairs. Outnumbered, enemy fighters broke off.

- 10th—Bletchley Park learned that Hitler had postponed invasion until September 21. Göring assured Hitler that the RAF would be defeated by then.

- 13th—Italian forces in Libya attacked Egypt. After a short advance, they halted to reorganize their supply lines. Churchill was apprised of the worsening situation in Egypt. Churchill's dispatch of 150 tanks seemed justified.

- 15th—The day the Battle of Britain turned. Bentley Priory learned of a massive attack of 328 bombers and 769 fighters or 80% of all fighter strength being sent across the Channel. All RAF fighters were thrown into battle. Luftwaffe pilots were shocked to see the RAF's fighter strength. Dowding put everything into the sky to demonstrate that RAF Fighter Command had not been destroyed. Churchill travelled to Group 11's operations centre at Uxbridge to see the battle unfold in real time on the map table. Churchill asked Park what reserves were left. "None" was the reply. At the end of the day, as Churchill left the centre, he muttered the words, "Never in the face of human conflict has so much been owed by so many to so few"[3] as he realized the true impact of the solution on the RAF.

  o Churchill was speechless as he realized Dowding's massive gamble, and all of his fighters were committed. Bentley Priory realized a second raid was afoot, and Dowding set a trap with multiple layers of fighters. By 2:30 pm, RAF refuelled, rearmed, and put up twenty squadrons once again to meet the Luftwaffe. For the first time, the RAF outnumbered the Luftwaffe. The second wave was beaten back, and the RAF destroyed 187 planes to break the offensive. Luftwaffe pilots were shocked at RAF's fighter strength, and their morale sapped. If a third wave had been sent out, then RAF would not have been able to defeat it.

Figure 25.2. September 15. (Courtesy of Crown copyright.)

- 17th—Bletchley Park decrypted orders to dismantle equipment at airfields. This was Hitler's order to postpone Operation Sea Lion. Churchill broadcast to the people of Czechoslovakia from Storey's Gate, "Be of good cheer, the time of your deliverance will come."[4] Churchill was a rallying voice.

- 18th—RAF bombers knocked out 150 barges, and Hitler cancelled Sea Lion.

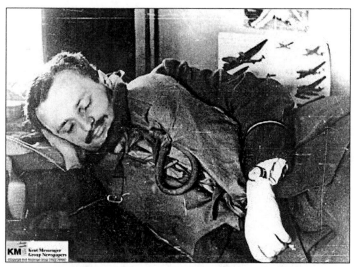

Figure 25.3. Exhausted pilots recoup on the 18th of September. (Courtesy of Crown copyright.)

- 21ˢᵗ—Churchill feared large civilian casualties from bombing raids. The London Underground was opened up at night and allowed for use as a bomb shelter.

- 24ᵗʰ—The Luftwaffe raids hit the vital Supermarine works at Woolston. Beaverbrook made plans for the further dispersal of production.

Figure 25.4. Luftwaffe fighters across the Channel on 24th of September. (Courtesy of Crown copyright.)

- 26th—Woolston was bombed again, severely damaging the factory and halting production. This resulted in the implementation of large-scale dispersal of production facilities to some sixty different sites.

- 28th—The last Luftwaffe daylight raid, but this was a major mistake. With no clouds, there were severe losses to Luftwaffe pilots.

Conclusion

By the end of September, the Luftwaffe switched to nighttime bombing. The RAF losses were 715 aircraft destroyed, 544 pilots were killed (1 in 5, where 1 in 4 pilots were from overseas). In comparison, the Luftwaffe losses were 900 aircraft destroyed and 3000 aircrew killed or taken prisoner. The battle ended in September, although it was a very close run thing. Beaverbrook's supply chain and Dowding's system were significant factors in the victory.

Did Churchill's solution meet the requirements and reach its goals? In this final period, the solution was providing the key players (Churchill, Beaverbrook, and Dowding) with critical information to improve their decision making, so they could better meet objectives. In particular, Beaverbrook had superseded expectations in fighter production for two months. The answer is a conclusive "yes."

Did the output achieve what it was designed to do? The last part of the battle almost resulted in defeat as the RAF was overwhelmed. However, with the real-time information from his system, Dowding was able to produce the knockout blow. The answer is a conclusive "yes."

Did it assist in a critical situation and help the organization react to it? It provided enemy intent, so the organization could react proactively and rapidly change tactics as required. The answer is a conclusive "yes."

Key Lessons

In today's projects:

- Agile leaders can move swiftly, more so than their rivals or competition.

- And:

- Risk Management (PMBoK KA)—

  o Review the risks in production. Collect metrics, and review these.

- Integration Management (PMBoK KA)—

  o Have back out plans ready in case of problems in production.

Educators

- How critical was the switch in Luftwaffe tactics?

CHAPTER TWENTY-SIX

Historical Events of October 1940— Summary of Air Battle

This chapter examines October 1940, what happened to Churchill's team, and the outcome of the story.

On October 12, Hitler abandoned Operation Sea Lion, the planned German invasion of Britain. By the end of October, the Battle of Britain was officially won. Winston Churchill believed that another invasion attempt was possible but only in March or April 1941.

Beaverbrook

By the end of October 1940, Beaverbrook's propaganda campaign, which urged the public to "Buy a Spitfire" through donations, helped build 1,000 aircraft and made people feel that they were part of the war effort, boosting morale.

By the end of 1940, British factories produced 4,283 fighters, compared to Germany's 3,000. In fact, so many aircraft were being produced that the United Kingdom could boast there were more fighter aircraft than pilots to fly them.

Month	Planned	Achieved	Overall Available
February	171	141	
March	203	177	
April	231	256	
May	261	325	
June	292	446	600
July	329	496	644
August	282	476	708
September			746
October			734

Figure 26.1. Monthly UK fighter production output, 1940.[1]

The CRO had played a significant role in this, and by the end of 1940, it had repaired 4,955 airframes, about 33% of the total airframe output going to the RAF. This can be seen in figure 26.2 with the fighters steadily increasing from storage units.

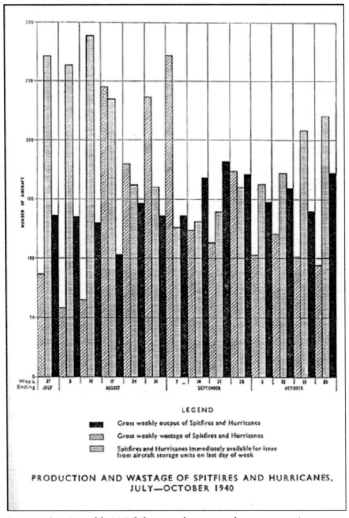

Figure 26.2. Monthly UK fighter production and wastage, 1940 (Courtesy of Crown copyright).

Beaverbrook continued to work with industrialists in North America. Significantly, another major achievement was his initiative with Pratt and Whitney to manufacture the Rolls

Royce engines. This did not materialize in time for the battle, although it led to the greatest fighter of the war—the P51 Mustang.

Dowding

Dowding was due for retirement on July 14 but delayed his retirement until the end of October. In October 1940, there was a post mortem of the Battle of Britain and Dowding (now aged 58) was under pressure for not using the big wing tactics developed by Group 12, which proved somewhat successful in the later stages of the battle. However, Leigh-Mallory, commander of Group 12, was not apprised of Ultra information, and Dowding was unable to defend his case without betraying Ultra to a junior officer, Douglas Baeder, sent by Leigh-Mallory. As a result, Dowding could not justify his position and relinquished his position as a new Chief of Air Staff (Air Chief Marshal Portal) took the post. Ironically, the man who had won the Battle of Britain was replaced by Leigh-Mallory. Dowding's career was not the last one sacrificed to keep Ultra secret. One lasting legacy was Dowding's creation at Bentley Priory. It went on to become the archetype for command-and-control centres around the world, and it is still used today. Its use of the filter room and real-time models through the map table and tote board were breakthroughs.

Bletchley Park

Although its role in the battle was limited to the order of battle for the German Air Force (GAF), by October, Churchill had become very reliant on the decrypts. The organization, with his support, continued to receive investments and grew to over 10,000 people by 1941. In the longer term, the overall knowledge-driven culture had a profound effect on the course of the war. It was the birthplace of the electronic intelligence and communications revolution, the cradle of the

Knowledge Age. It was a community that dramatically pushed emerging technology to its limits and created the first working, programmable electronic computer, Colossus, in 1943. It provided a glimpse into the future we see today. Bletchley Park was completely dismantled and eradicated after the war to preserve the Ultra secret, which was not revealed until 1974.

Churchill

In the closing stages of the battle, Churchill had spent critical time with U.S. journalists based in London. Churchill was able to focus on his long-term objectives, specifically in drawing the U.S. closer to the United Kingdom. By autumn, Lord Lothian (UK ambassador to the U.S.) was able to report that the Battle of Britain and London's toughness had inspired a renewal of American confidence in British nerve and strength. The policy of "defending America by helping Britain" was now "really representative of average American opinion, and for the first time the British became popular in America."

Beyond October 1940

The Luftwaffe switched to nighttime attacks, the blitz of London continued into May 1941, and it was extended to other cities. The goal was to bomb England into submission.

Figure 26.3. Blitz on St. Paul's. (Courtesy of Crown copyright.).

The bombing did not have the desired effect on the civilian population and just further hardened British resolve.

Figure 26.4. Blitz continues into 1941. (Courtesy of Crown copyright.)

During this period, the Luftwaffe losses were staggering—2,700 aircraft were destroyed and 600 damaged. British losses were about 1140 fighters or 900 pilots. In June 1941, Hitler turned his attention to the Soviet Union and an invasion of Britain was scrapped.

Conclusion

Even though the RAF was badly mauled, it remained intact to repel raids. RAF had warning of about 80% of air raids on London. In addition, the supply chain had adequately supported RAF to sustain prolonged air battle. The Luftwaffe loss of 2700 aircrew, the best they had, never recovered from this and had a significant impact on the Russian campaign.

Churchill weathered the storm and turned the corner meeting all short- and long-term objectives. He was defiant, full of confidence, and able to implement longer-term strategies.

Most authors and historians agree that the Battle of Britain had a significant effect on the course of the war. It changed the conduct of war, as it showed the Allies how a sense-and-respond system could be leveraged to turn the course of the battle and the importance of agility. As a result, the use of intelligence became the top priority over everything, including other military resources.

Key Lessons

In today's projects:

- Agile leaders see the big picture and are not limited by a short-term view.

And:

- Cost Management (PMBoK KA)—
    - Collect metrics to determine the success of the cost benefit analysis (CBA) and the solution.

Educators

- How sound was Churchill's decision to spend critical time with U.S. journalists?
- How successful was the solution in the end?

CHAPTER TWENTY-SEVEN

Conclusion, Wrap Up, and Takeaways

This final chapter reviews the book's key points, the transformation project and solution, and a summary of lessons in agile leadership. The intent is to give you the reader takeaways for your projects (transformation) and ideas for what you can do.

Agile leadership is important in today's world as organizations face an increasing environment of continuous change. One of the principal characteristics of an adaptive organization is its resilience to ride out changes, and this requires flexibility and agility.

To overcome limited institutional agility, key factors required include *leadership, culture and values, and an effective organizational process for the management of change.* However, institutional agility, exemplified by rapid innovation and adoption, causes anxiety in the organization and resistance to change and builds barriers to the process of learning.

Through the book, the characteristics of agile leaders were introduced. Let's review Churchill's characteristics and background and how this influenced him to operate in what can be described today as an agile leader and turning his organization agile.

Takeaway #1—look for opportunities to establish credibility

The story starts prior to Churchill becoming PM and taking on the project. The whole of Churchill's previous career had been a preparation for wartime leadership. He was a historian who understood early on in the 1930s what was happening on the world stage with the rise of fascism. With a long political exile, he was astute enough to maximize the impact of valuable information he had collected and build up his case for responding to the threat with proactive actions. He recognized that one of the chief goals of a leader is to rally people to a cause and to do that requires considerable credibility gained through *portraying self-belief, steadfastness, and integrity to a cause.* "An appeaser is one who feeds a crocodile, hoping it will eat him last."[1]

Takeaway #2—formulate how to approach a PM position and actions to take

Churchill was a politician and therefore more adaptable to changing situations. He could read the mood of the people and respond. Churchill saw the PM position somewhat differently, possibly as an opportunity at least to try something different. In May 1940, senior politicians moved away from the position because of the "no win" situation associated with it. In contrast, he had already *formulated in his mind how he would approach the position and what he would do.* Early on, he recognized he needed full authority to have a reasonable chance of success.

Takeaway #3—communicate and then reinforce the vision for change

A change in mindset is required to overcome the resistance to organizational agility. Agile leaders must *stimulate the organizational realization that change is constant, that the transformation project is a dynamic journey and not a static destination,* and that the consequences of inaction are worse than action. Many transformation projects are often instigated in a "back to the wall situation," where the outcome is critical to the success or even survival of the business, with little elbowroom for the schedule. This was the situation for the United Kingdom in 1940. Agile leaders should constantly communicate and then reinforce the vision for change as part of the management of change process. They also need to participate in and monitor the transformation project that catalyses the change, so they can measure its success.

Takeaway #4 – create contingencies for worst-case scenarios

Churchill showed the depth of his commitment to the project from the outset by decisions he made. He did not panic and faced difficulties such as Dunkirk face on. The situation was disastrous, but Churchill kept his *composure and his resolve; he stuck to a plan to continue to find a resolution to the most pressing problems.*

Churchill was managing a deteriorating and desperate situation. He had to make a monumental decision to stand and fight, rather than evacuate, so as not to strain the Allied relationship further. Churchill was fighting for the survival of the project. Fortunately, he had *contingency plans in place.* "Success is the ability to go from one failure to another with no loss of enthusiasm."[2]

Churchill also put his position as PM at considerable risk. He walked a tightrope in that he could have been ejected from power following Dunkirk. Instead, he pulled off one of the most significant speeches of the whole war and that of his life. In this one speech, not only did he boost morale but set out his priorities. This was leadership at the finest, and Churchill's prestige was elevated, as was his resolution to keep going.

Takeaway #5—create a communication plan and stick to it

Churchill and Alfred Duff Cooper had turned Dunkirk into a propaganda victory, particularly with the role of the "little boats." In fact, the spin was almost too successful, setting off a wave of public euphoria in which a gallant loser escapes from disaster at the last moment. This was important, as the news was not going to get any better. *In today's world, we call this a communication plan.*

Churchill's speeches are legendary. However, oratory did not come naturally to Churchill; he had to study and practice it. He never gave a speech from memory and would spend days preparing it. He liked short words, believing they would be better understood. He also used statistics as cold-blooded facts in getting his point across and underlining key aspects.

Takeaway #6—show preparedness where possible

Churchill hated negative thinking, procrastination, tentativeness, second-guessing, second-hand information, and advisory committees. He wanted to show preparedness (material, moral, practical, and psychological) for all eventualities and pushed for actions that reflected that.

He was a devotee of action who thrived on challenge and crisis, a man of iron constitution, inexhaustible energy, and total concentration. He established a culture that took the fight forward where possible. For example, he set up the Commandos. He also set the order not to sit, but to drive the Axis out of East and North Africa.

Takeaway #7—create both short- and long-term strategies

Churchill pushed *a tactical to strategic transition by laying out a strategy that he immediately enabled.* He defined a vision and set out a short- and long-term strategy to win the war. As part of the short-term strategy (two months):

- He had to restore confidence in his project and the will to fight on within his cabinet, government, and the public.

- He had to inspire his nation to continue a fight already considered lost, win the air battle, and stall the invasion until spring 1941.

"It is a mistake to try to look too far ahead. The chain of destiny can only be grasped one link at a time,"[3] As part of the long-term strategy (up to five to seven years), he had to

- Quickly move the peacetime economy to a war footing.

- Expand the war through an alliance with the U.S.

- Bring hope to Nazi-occupied Europe and to the free world.

Takeaway #8—ensure adequate governance is in place to get groups working

Churchill had been the Minister for War Production in the First World War and responsible for scaling up tank manufacturing, a technology that could have enormous impact on trench warfare. He oversaw the production of over 350 tanks, enough for a large-scale offensive at Cambrai. He had seen firsthand *the importance of closely aligning industry (civilian) with military demand under government auspices.*

Churchill, conscious of the mistakes of the Great War realized that he needed full authority to have a reasonable chance of success, and this required a governance framework. Churchill broke down the barriers between vertical organizations through a revised governance framework. He *deconstructed and reconstructed silos.* He kept the War Cabinet size to a manageable eight and combined his job as prime minister with that of the Minister of Defence.

Churchill was also a military man, having served in the Army and Navy. He understood the military organization, mind, and culture. He united these organizations, which coexisted in bitter rivalry, harnessing their energies in the same direction to fight for the same cause. Churchill with the chiefs of staff embedded in the War Cabinet was the core of the system and a war-winning framework. The *Grand War Strategy*, as it was known, was run in a rational and logical way with checks and balances.

Takeaway #9—listen to experts when they present ideas and solutions, and enact these

One of Churchill's great personal strengths was that he listened to his experts, the scientists and technologists, when they presented their ideas and solutions to him. He embraced emerging technology, understood, applied, and adopted it—from the first tanks in 1917 to radar in 1938.

As a long-standing and skillful politician, Churchill knew the mechanics and politics of government. As a wartime prime minister, he had a lot of power. He could navigate around the "mandarins" and civil servants of the ministries, knowing which strings to pull, and enable change.

Takeaway #10—select team leaders who are not afraid to challenge you

Churchill was able to recognize the brilliant mavericks, such as Beaverbrook and Dowding, and bring them to the forefront. He had the foresight to *allow them to get on with it*. He backed them when needed, helping remove all obstacles in their paths. "He [Winston Churchill] delegated freely but also probed and interfered continuously, regarding nothing as too large or too small for his attention." [4]

These *leaders were able to stand up to Churchill and challenge him*. They brought in best practices from various industries and used metrics to track and guide the project. Beaverbrook, an outsider, took a very different approach to the supply chain and introduced the basic concepts of agility. Beaverbrook's approach aimed to solve the problems holistically by bringing in qualified industry leaders, securing raw materials, resolving labour issues, and building public good will.

On the other hand, Dowding, with his open and enquiring mind, built the RAF Fighter Command structure around the "Dowding System," sophisticated institutionalized decision making that used real-time event models. With a sophisticated early-warning system, it was the first time information had been used on such an industrial scale. The tracking of wastage and the ability to direct Beaverbrook's

Civilian Repair Operation helped turn the course of the Battle of Britain. Dowding was recognized by the enemy and was number 3 on Hitler's assassination list.

Takeaway #11—look for people who are resilient to constant change and who adjust to new situations quickly

In today's projects, specifically those that cross organizational boundaries, finding the right mix of people for the project team is a prerequisite for success. Leaders need to be flexible, agile, and react to situations that impact a project and factors that affect a project. As pointed out in *The Resilience Factor* by Bob Weinstein, "Highly resilient people are best suited for a world of constant change." They do not fight against disruptive change because they adjust to new situations quickly. Often players from across the organization are needed to help with adoption and buy-in.

Churchill recognized that one of the chief goals of a leader was to understand changes and be proactive and agile in dealing with these. This needs not just information but insight and knowledge. Core to Churchill's solution was gaining insight and intelligence into the rapidity and impact of change. For Churchill, "knowledge was, indeed, power," and Bletchley Park provided priceless insights into the strategic thinking and tactical intent of the enemy. Although these were early days for Bletchley Park, its importance grew, and it could be attributed with shortening the duration of the war by two years.

Takeaway #12—continually project confidence and resolve to the cause

Churchill's greatest personal achievement was projecting confidence and resolve to the cause. This was when most people were ready to give up. He did this not just through his speeches but his actions. In other words, he acted courageously to shift the mood and bolster morale. In today's world, morale is essential to a working project; it can make or break it.

Churchill was able create a unique identity, a brand, the "bulldog," based on his tenacity and resolve to cause. In today's world, organizations strive to create a brand and experience based on core values.

Final takeaway, a summary of AGILE characteristics that were exemplified by Churchill:

- Agile leaders portray self-belief, steadfastness, and integrity to a cause.

- Agile leaders are well-informed; they read, study, and seek challenging assignments.

- Agile leaders display honesty, sincerity, integrity, and candour in all their actions.

- Agile leaders take competent actions based on reason and moral principles (the balanced decision-making approach at Storey's Gate).

- Agile leaders are forward-looking, can set objectives, and have a vision of the future that the organization can adopt (Churchill's short- and long-term strategies). They position for the continual and sustained success of the organization.

- Agile leaders move quickly and iteratively, with agility, once the vision is clear (response to Dunkirk).

- Agile leaders are inspiring, willing to take risks, and display confidence in all that they do (this was most spectacularly seen at Oran where Churchill took the most pivotal actions).

- Agile leaders are fair-minded and show fair treatment to everyone (Churchill's reaction to Dowding's letter).

- Agile leaders look for sub-leaders that can challenge the status quo and are unafraid to go out on a limb (like Beaverbrook).

- Agile leaders are broad-minded; they seek out adversity of viewpoints and opinions.

- Agile leaders are courageous and have the perseverance to reach an objective, even with seemingly insurmountable obstacles (Churchill's pursuit of long-term strategy).

- Agile leaders simplify complex situations (through tools) and use sound judgments to make good decisions at the right time.

- Agile leaders are imaginative and, based on the situation, can make timely and appropriate changes in their thinking, plans, and methods.

- Agile leaders encourage creative thinking of new and better goals, ideas, and solutions to problems (Churchill pushed his cabinet for ideas). They reward achievement, innovation, and change.

Summary

Based on all this information, it is easy to understand why Churchill was such a great leader,[5] and he was recognized for it in 1940.[6] It would have been all too easy to go with the majority of the establishment, sue for peace, and set up a "Vichy England." Instead, Churchill resolutely went against massive pressure and put up a fight that eventually led his nation to victory. In summary, Churchill's agility transformed the United Kingdom through a transformation project, so it could "adapt to change" and become agile.

Profiles

Churchill

Winston Churchill's daily routine helped him function with "agility" and manage his transformation project. He was working with a time-constrained project, so how did he, as a leader, pace and pattern his day? How did he maximize his working day efficiency? What were his work habits and work style? Churchill was a workaholic and his workday was organized to fit two full eight-hour days in a twenty-four-hour period.

- 0800 am—Woke up, had a sizeable breakfast, and worked from his bed. He read his mail and papers from his prime ministerial box. He also dictated to his secretaries and held discussions with his senior military advisors.

- 1000 am—First chiefs of staff meeting.

- 1200 pm—War Cabinet meeting. A second meeting could be held later.

- 1700 pm—Back to bed for deep sleep.

- 1900 pm—Woke up to start second shift.

- 2000 pm—Dinner meetings were important to Churchill. They were dominated by table talk, which was as important as the meal. Sometimes, depending on the company, drinks and cigars extended the event well past midnight.

- 2200 pm—As dinner guests retired, Churchill continued to work, reading briefs from his study.

- 0000 am—Review of all the main daily national newspapers, looking for trends and public opinion.

Churchill was very aware, firsthand, of the value of good intelligence. Lack of it had been a major undoing for him at Gallipoli during the First World War. Therefore, he looked for specific information and intelligence:

- He supported Ultra, the code-breaking establishment at Bletchley Park.

- He had a personal daily briefing of significant Ultra decrypts. These greatly influenced his overall strategy.

- He demanded to see secret intelligence material in the raw that was unfiltered by aides.

- He read telegrams, both service and diplomatic. The former were sent between the chiefs of staff and commanders in the field, the latter by the Foreign Office to ambassadors.

- He collected periodic returns, monthly/weekly/daily reports on production and technical developments.

Churchill had the highest possible level of knowledge accumulated, and these secret worlds of intelligence and deception played a critical aspect in his decisions.

Churchill was a team player, and he drew help and inspiration from those around him. He augmented his own personal decision making by surrounding himself with professionals. He surrounded himself by the best team he could (knowledge through people and solutions), for example:

- Typists (three)—all his thoughts and sayings were recorded.

- Private secretaries—worked a twenty-four-hour rota system.

- Private secretariat at 10 Downing Street.

- Daily contact with the Head of Intelligence Stewart Menzies.

- Access to experts, the best possible professionals, e.g., Professor Lindemann was the head of Churchill's Statistical Office for interpretation. He was appointed for his statistical expertise to examine information from government ministries and the supply chain.

- Churchill built a very close relationship with the chiefs of staff through daily meetings.

- "He delegated freely but also probed and interfered continuously, regarding nothing as too large or too small for his attention." [1]

- He introduced the system of "action this day." These famous stickers were attached to his memos.

Churchill's war[2] continued, and his long-term objective was met when the U.S. entered the war in December 1941. After this point, the tide turned with a few hiccups on the way.

In 1945, the war ended, and the Labour Party was swept into power on the euphoria of optimism and expected social change. Churchill's career never again reached its wartime peak, although he became a peacetime prime minister in 1951 at the age of 76. In 1965, he died and had a state funeral reserved for the greatest Britons.

Storey's Gate

Today, the Storey's Gate complex is intact and operates as a museum. It was completely closed down and mothballed on the last day of the war. Nothing was removed or changed, so the map room still has the indicators for industrial production and the orders of battle for the last days of the war.

Beaverbrook

Certainly, he was as effective in politics as he was in business, the confidante of Prime Ministers Winston Churchill and David Lloyd George (from whom his peerage was awarded). He became a British press lord, blazing the trail for other colonials, such as fellow Canadian Roy Thomson and the Australian Rupert Murdoch. He bought—and sold— automaker Rolls Royce. At its height, his *Daily Express* had a circulation of close to four million, and he made no bones about using his newspapers to push his or his friends' agendas.[3]

In 1940, the new Prime Minister had long regarded Beaverbrook as a confidant, and now, a very necessary addition to the war effort. The minister's irascible zeal soon proved its worth. Fighter and bomber production were immeasurably increased. "This was his hour, His personal force and genius, combined with so much persuasion and contrivance, swept aside many obstacles. Everything in the supply line was drawn forward to the battle…" Not many people in Beaverbrook's ministries enjoyed being treated like his newspaper staff, and of course, he could not understand why, reflecting his character. As minister, he persistently complained of the difficulties that he faced. He fired off many letters of resignation until, finally, one was accepted. In September 1943, he was back as Lord Privy Seal, for Churchill could not live without his counsel,[4] despite all their differences.

Dowding

Air Chief Marshal Sir Hugh Dowding, Air Officer Commanding-in-Chief Fighter Command was born at Moffat in 1882. Educated at Winchester and the Royal Military Academy, Woolwich, he was commissioned in the Royal Garrison Artillery, and he spent the early years of his service career overseas. After spending two years at the Staff College, Camberley, Dowding took the opportunity to learn to fly at Brooklands and gained his RFC wings during 1913.

The outbreak of the Great War saw him spend time in France with Nos. 6 and 9 Squadrons before his interest in wireless telegraphy led to him to return home to form the Wireless Experimental Establishment at Brooklands in April 1915. Within months, however, Dowding was back in France, this time as Officer Commanding No. 16 Squadron before taking command of the Ninth (Headquarters) Wing during the Battle of the Somme. Differences of opinion with Trenchard saw him return to the United Kingdom to run the Southern Training Brigade at Salisbury, a post he occupied for the rest of the war.

Following the war, Dowding spent time in the Air Ministry and in staff officer posts, but his appointment at the Air Council as Air Member for Supply and Research at the end of 1930 and his subsequent position as Air Member for Research and Development influenced the future shape of Britain's defences. Here, he encouraged the development of advanced fighter aircraft, and it was largely on his initiative that the Hurricane and Spitfire were ordered into production in 1934. He also showed tremendous interest in the detection of enemy aircraft and provided his full support to the new Radio Direction Finding (RDF) equipment then under development.

His interest in defence made him the natural choice to command the new Fighter Command when it was set up in July 1936 and was disappointed to be overlooked for the position of Chief of the Air Staff (CAS) in 1937 (which went to Newall). Dowding continued to prepare his command for war, overseeing the introduction of new aircraft, bulletproof windscreens, the development of the Observer Corps, and the integration of RDF units with communications and control organisations into a structure far in advance of anything else in the world.

Heavy fighter losses in France saw Dowding warn the War Cabinet of the dire consequences should the present wastage rates continue, and a letter dated 16 May 1940 is one of the great documents of history. After covering the evacuation from Dunkirk, he had just enough aircraft to fight the Luftwaffe in the one place they could be effectively used—within the comprehensive air defence system he had built in the United Kingdom. Even so, he admitted that the situation was "critical in the extreme," and while it is true that the immortal "Few"—his "chicks" as Churchill christened them—won the battle using the organisation he had created, the Luftwaffe lost it through bad leadership, faulty tactics, and mistaken target selection. His personal role was, of course, limited. Day-to-day control of the fighters rested with the group commanders, of which Air Vice-Marshal Park (11 Group) and Air Vice-Marshal Leigh-Mallory (12 Group) bore the brunt of the enemy attacks. However, the differing views of the two men (Park's closely matched those of Dowding, while Leigh-Mallory favoured large formations of defending aircraft—"big wings") and Dowding's inability to settle the squabble between the two led to serious criticism of him. The Air Ministry favoured Leigh-Mallory's policies, and Dowding was increasingly seen as uncooperative and difficult to get on with. Within weeks of the end of the Battle of Britain and with a new CAS (Air Chief Marshal Portal) in post, Dowding (now aged fifty-eight) relinquished his position. Churchill persuaded him to head an aircraft-purchasing mission to the U.S., a role for which he was quite unsuited, and he headed a major RAF economy study before finally retiring in July 1942.

An unwillingness to break with service precedents meant that Dowding was not promoted to the rank of Marshal of the Royal Air Force—even when it was suggested by the king, and he spent the rest of his life largely away from the RAF. In later years, he became president of the Battle of Britain Fighter Association. After his death in 1970, his remains were interred in Westminster Abbey, a fitting tribute to his remarkable achievements.

In the short term, Ultra had a profound effect on the United Kingdom's defence strategies and the course of the Battle of Britain by providing early warning of enemy intent, strength, size of raids, and their timing. For example, RAF Fighter Command was aware of massive enemy attacks (i.e., Eagle Day—August 13, 1940) and any changes in enemy tactics. Dowding was receiving two hundred to three hundred decoded messages a day.

Bentley Priory[5] Fighter Command Headquarters

Prior to the outbreak of World War II in 1939, the Priory suffered many changes. Chief among these was the hurried adaptation of the two largest rooms (now the Anteroom and the Ladies Room) into the Operations Room and the Filter Room—moved from its original location in the Crypt Bar; the classrooms in the East Wing were converted into accommodations.

In January 1939, work started on the underground Operations Block, which was occupied, and it commenced operations on 9 March 1940. The average depth of the excavations was forty-two feet. It contained the Operations and Filter Rooms, the essential elements of the command, control, and communications system that became the cornerstone of the Air Defence System. The system allowed the controllers the best chance to ensure that they could always respond to incoming raids by scrambling squadrons to intercept them before they reached their targets. This rapid, flexible reaction was essential, as there were insufficient aircraft and crews to mount standing patrols.

Bentley Priory continued to act as the Headquarters of Fighter Command throughout the war and assumed additional importance as the planning headquarters for D-Day. On D-Day, the King George VI, Winston Churchill, and General Eisenhower monitored the landings in the Allied Expeditionary Air Force War Room in the underground bunker. The German artillery binoculars on display in the Dowding Room were brought back on the C-in-C's orders, having been captured from positions overlooking the beaches in France.

Uxbridge Group 11 Headquarters of Fighter Command

During the Battle of Britain, Group 11 was responsible for the defence of London, the Southeast of England, and the main areas of combat. It remained in operation for a while, and then it was completely closed down and mothballed. Today, it is intact and operates as a private museum.

Observer Corps

The Observer Corps won its spurs during the Battle of Britain and in his dispatch, Lord Dowding said, "It is important to note that, at this time the Observer Corps constituted the whole means of tracking enemy raids once they had crossed the coastline, their work throughout was quite invaluable, without it, air raid warning systems could not have been operated and inland interceptions would rarely have been made. In recognition of the invaluable work done by the Observer Corps, an announcement was made in the House of Commons on 9 April 1941 that His Majesty King George VI had granted the Corps the title "Royal."

Air Vice-Marshal Sir Keith Park, Air Officer Commanding 11 Group

A New Zealander, and son of Professor James Park, Keith Park came to Britain to serve in the First World War as a gunner before transferring to the Royal Flying Corps during 1917 and receiving a permanent commission in the Royal Air Force.

He was given command of his first squadron on 10 April 1918, 48 Squadron, the first to be equipped with the Bristol Fighter, and later passed through the RAF Staff College before being appointed air attaché to Argentina. By 1938, he had become Dowding's right-hand man as senior staff officer in Fighter Command, and he was subsequently appointed Air Officer Commanding No 11 Group. Like his commander, Park was relieved of his post almost immediately after the Battle of Britain and given command of a flying training group. This was the outcome of pointed criticism of his tactics by Leigh-Mallory, Air Officer Commanding No. 12 Group, who had gained favour within the War Cabinet and disliked both Dowding and his ally, Park.

In 1942, he became Air Officer Commanding Malta. This was during the anxious period in which the defence of the island rested with a few Hurricanes that fought with great determination and courage until the arrival of additional aircraft and aid allowed the garrison to be saved and the Mediterranean cleared. In January 1944, he was appointed Air Officer Commander-in-Chief Middle East and, a year later, Allied Air Commander-in-Chief of Southeast Asia Command. He died, aged 82, in New Zealand in 1975. It has been said of him by one of the great fighter leaders of the Second World War, Air Vice-Marshal "Johnnie"Johnson, that "he was the only man who could have lost the war in a day or even an afternoon."

President Franklin Delano Roosevelt

Roosevelt shifted his stance towards the United Kingdom prior to and during 1940. Bound by the Neutrality Act, he walked a tightrope of direct support. He boosted Churchill's morale while keeping him a certain distance. Seemingly sympathetic, he was cautious and suspicious of Churchill. He was at odds with British imperial tendencies and the British Empire. Below is the timeline of U.S. entry into the war:

- 1940 July 19—President Roosevelt signs the Two-Ocean Navy Expansion Act, ordering construction of 1.3 million tons of new warships and 15,000 naval planes.

- 1940 September 2—Roosevelt passes the Destroyers for Bases Agreement to give fifty American destroyers to the United Kingdom in exchange for military base rights in the British Caribbean islands and Newfoundland.

- 1940 September 26—President Roosevelt embargoes U.S. export of scrap iron and steel.

- 1940 November 5—President Roosevelt is re-elected for an unprecedented third term.

- 1940 December 17—President Roosevelt gives a press conference announcing a Lend-Lease Bill, proposing massive aid for Great Britain in its war against Germany. Many, including the Germans, view this as a clear violation of American neutrality.

- 1940 December 29—President Roosevelt, in one of his famous "fireside" chats, tells the American people that he wishes the United States to become the "arsenal of democracy" and to give full aid to Britain regardless of threats from other countries.[6]

- 1941 March—the U.S. Congress passed the Lend-Lease Act giving the United Kingdom, the Republic of China, and later, the Soviet Union (June) $50 billion of military supplies between 1941–45.

1941 August 14, Roosevelt met with Churchill to develop the Atlantic Charter. The program developed estimates for the mobilization of labour, industry, and logistics to defeat the enemies of the United States. It also planned to have ten million men in arms, with five million ready for action abroad in 1943.

Herman Göring

Göring was the commander-in-chief of the Luftwaffe, and he personally directed the first attacks on the United Kingdom from his private luxury train. Göring's strategy was to entice RAF Fighter Command into major air battle. With superior numbers, he could grind out a victory in a battle of attrition. Even though he was held in high esteem and second in command to Hitler, he had a divide-and-rule approach to management and paid too little attention to detail. As this strategy faltered, he seized the opportunity to refocus on bombing London, squandering the chance to defeat the RAF..

London 1940

London was the heart of the largest and most prosperous empire that had reached its peak in 1940. London was the largest city in the world with a population of 8 million vs. Berlin's 4.34 million, New York's 5 million, and Paris' 2.5 million. London covered 100 square miles and was the home of the British monarchy and the centre of government and the British establishment. In commercial terms, it was also the financial capital, and a major port with substantial docks and warehouses. It also was a major seat of manufacturing and production, and the heart of both rail network, and canals. It had an extensive transportation system underground and over ground. It housed great institutions like museums, colleges, and universities. It was the heart of media newspapers and television. Little wonder that London became an important target for the Luftwaffe and changed the course of the battle.

Photo Credits

The illustrations on the cover, the frontispiece, and in Figure 6.3 were used courtesy of the Imperial War Museum, London.

Figures 5.1, 5.2, 8.1, 17.1, 17.2, 17.3, 19.1, 19.2, 19.3, 19.4, 20.10, 23.1, 23.2, 24.1, 25.1, 25.2, 25.3, 25.4, 26.2, 26.3, and 26.4 are provided courtesy of Crown Copyright, London.

Figures 3.1, 11.1, and 24.2 are provided courtesy of *Illustrated London News*.

Figures 12.1 and 15.1 are provided courtesy of the U.S. Library of Congress.

Figures 17.7, 19.5, 19.8, 19.12, and 24.3 are provided courtesy of Kent Messenger Group Newspaper.

Photos 19.15, 19.16, 20.1, 20.5, 20.6, 20.7, 20.8 and 20.9 are by Nick Kozak. Used with permission.

End Notes

Foreword

[1] Basil Collier, *Leader of the Few: The Authorised Biography of Air Chief Marshall, the Lord Dowding of Bentley Priory, G. C. B., G. C. V. O., C. M. G.* (London: Jarrolds, 1957), 103.

[2] Chief of the Air Staff Hugh Trenchard helped establish the Royal Air Force in 1918.

[3] Hugh Dowding, "Letter to the Air Ministry," May 16, 1940, Spartacus Educational, http://www.spartacus.schoolnet.co.uk/2WWdowding.htm.

Preface

[1] PMBoK KAs include integration management, scope Management, time management, cost management, quality management, HR management, risk management, and procurement management.

[2] Alvin and Heidi Toffler, Revolutionary Wealth: *How It Will Be Created and How It Will Change Our Lives* (New York: Alfred A. Knopf, 2006), 45.

Chapter 1

[1] BBC News: World Edition, "Churchill Voted Greatest Briton," November 22, 2004, http://news.bbc.co.uk/2/hi/entertainment/2509465.stm.

[2] Winston Churchill, "The Few," August 20, 1940, The Churchill Centre: Speeches & Quotes, http://www.winstonchurchill.org/i4a/pages/index.cfm?pageid=388#so_much_owed.

Chapter 3

[1] Winston Churchill, "The War Situation: House of Many Mansions," January 20, 1940, The Churchill Centre: Speeches & Quotes, http://www.winstonchurchill.org/i4a/pages/index.cfm?pageid=390&textonly=1.

Chapter 4

[1] Winston Churchill, "Blood, Toil, Tears and Sweat," May 13, 1940, The Churchill Centre: Speeches & Quotes, http://www.winstonchurchill.org/i4a/pages/index.cfm?pageid=391.

Chapter 5

[1] Paul Reynaud, May 1940, quoted in Julian Jackson, *The Fall Of France: The Nazi Invasion of 1940 (Making of the Modern World)* (New York: Oxford University Press, 2003).

[2] Winston Churchill, 1940, quoted in Julian Jackson, *The Fall Of France: The Nazi Invasion of 1940 (Making of the Modern World)* (New York: Oxford University Press, 2003).

Chapter 6

[1] Winston Churchill, "Be Ye Men of Valour," May 19, 1940, The Churchill Centre: Speeches & Quotes, http://www.winstonchurchill.org/i4a/pages/index. cfm?pageid=392&textonly=1.

Chapter 7

[1] Chiefs of staff, May 1940, quoted in Michael M. Postan, "From Dunkirk to Pearl Harbor," British War Production (London: HMSO, 1952), http:// www.ibiblio.org/hyperwar/UN/UK/UK-Civil-WarProduction/UK-Civil-WarProduction-4.html.

[2] Winston Churchill, May 1940, quoted in John Lukacs, "Half-Breed American," Five Days in London: May 1940, (New Haven, CT: Yale University Press, 2001). http://www.winstonchurchill.org/i4a/pages/index. cfm?pageid=686.

Chapter 8

[1] Ibid.

[2] Winston Churchill, "We Shall Fight on the Beaches," June 4, 1940, The Churchill Centre: Speeches & Quotes, http://www.winstonchurchill.org/i4a/pages/index. cfm?pageid=393.

[3] Josiah Wedgwood, quoted in Martin Gilbert, *Churchill: A Life* (London: Pimlico, 2000, 656).

[4] Winston Churchill, "We Shall Fight on the Beaches," June 4, 1940, The Churchill Centre: Speeches & Quotes, http://www.winstonchurchill.org/i4a/pages/index. cfm?pageid=393.

Chapter 9

[1] Encyclopedia Britannica Online, s.v. "Churchill, Winston," http://www.britannica.com/EBchecked/topic/117269/ Sir-Winston-Churchill/60595/As-prime-minister.

[2] Winston Churchill, quoted in Martin Gilbert, *Continue To Pester, Nag and Bite: Churchill's War Leadership* (London: Pimlico, 2005).

Chapter 10

[1] *International Journal of Software Engineering and Its Applications 2, no. 3* (2008), http://www.sersc.org/ journals/IJSEIA/vol2_no3_2008/8.pdf.

[2] John Colville, *The Fringes of Power: The Incredible Inside Story Of Winston Churchill During WWII (Guilford*, CT: The Lyons Press, 2002).

[3] Initiated May 17 because of priorities.

[4] W.K. Hancock and M. M. Gowing, "Organisation at the Centre," in *British War Economy* (London: HMSO, 1949).

Chapter 13

[1] Duncan Anderson, "Spinning Dunkirk," February 6, 2004, BBC World Wars: World War Two, http://www. bbc.co.uk/history/worldwars/wwtwo/dunkirk_ spinning_01.shtml.

Chapter 14

[1] Although documentation in cabinet minutes is sparse, the Campaign (Churchill's Communication Plan) can be pieced together from newspapers, recordings, and transcripts of radio programs.

[2] Winston Churchill, quoted in "Datelines," 2001, The Churchill Centre: Publications & Resources, http://www.winstonchurchill.org/i4a/pages/index. cfm?pageid=288.

[3] Barton Biggs, *Wealth, War and Wisdom* (Hoboken, NJ: John Wiley & Sons, Inc., 2008).

[4] Winston Churchill, quoted in Martin Gilbert, Continue to Pester, Nag and Bite: Churchill's War Leadership (London: Pimlico, 2005).

[5] Winston Churchill, quoted in John Charmley, *Churchill: The End of Glory: A Political Biography* (New York: Harcourt Brace, 1994).

[6] Jennifer James, Ph.D., "Becoming an Adaptive Leader," (presented at the 27th Management Forum Series, October 4, 2006), http://www.executiveforum.com/PDFs/JamesSynopsis.pdf.

Chapter 15

[1] BBC, The BBC at War 1939–1945: Reporting the War, http://www.bbc.co.uk/heritage/story/ww2/reporting. shtml.

[2] Winston Churchill, *Their Finest Hour* (Boston: Houghton Mifflin, 1949).

[3] W.K. Hancock and M. M. Gowing, "If Necessary for Years, If Necessary Alone," *in British War Economy* (London: HMSO, 1949).

[4] Chiefs of staff, May 1940, quoted in Michael M. Postan, "From Dunkirk to Pearl Harbor," *British War Production* (London: HMSO, 1952), http://www.ibiblio.org/hyperwar/UN/UK/UK-Civil-WarProduction/UK-Civil-WarProduction-4.html.

[5] "Sir Winston Churchill and the War in Europe," Ebeneezer's Library, http://www.personal.psu.edu/users/t/u/tuh125/churchill.html.

[6] Winston Churchill, quoted in "How Churchill Did It," 2001, The Churchill Centre: Publications & Resources, http://www.winstonchurchill.org/i4a/pages/index.cfm?pageid=283.

Chapter 16

[1] Winston Churchill, quoted in A. D. Harvey, *Collision of Empires: Britain in Three World Wars, 1793–1945* (London: Hambledon & London, 2003).

Chapter 17

[1] Lord Beaverbrook, quoted in "Resource Mobilization for World War II: the U.S.A., U. K., U. S. S. R., and Germany, 1938–1945," *Economic History Review*, 41, no. 2, (2008): 171–192.

[2] In 1938, the automobile industry worldwide totaled 4 Million. The U.S. produced 2.5 million units. The United Kingdom, the second largest producer, produced just fewer than 9% or 445,000 units.

[3] Lord Beaverbrook, quoted in "Historical Perspectives," The Worker's War: Home Front Recalled, http://www.unionhistory.info/workerswar/browse.php?irn=317.

⁴ Frank Winters, PMP, "The Top Ten Reasons Projects Fail (Part 4)," *Gantthead*, April 16, 2003.

Chapter 18

¹ Ultra information was screened and passed indirectly to Dowding by his superiors; he was not fully apprised of the source until October 1940.

² Winston Churchill, quoted in "UK: Codebreaking HQ Becomes a Theme Park," June 10, 1999, BBC News, http://news.bbc.co.uk/2/hi/uk_news/365944.stm.

³ Further information on Bletchley Park: http://www.bletchleypark.org.uk/.

Chapter 19

¹ A total of 1,029 aircraft and over 1,500 personnel.

² Hugh Dowding, quoted in M. W. Kirby, *Operational Research In War and Peace: The British Experience from the 1930s to 1970* (London: Imperial College Press, 2003).

³ Ultra information was first screened and passed indirectly To Dowding by his superiors; he was not fully apprised of the source until October 1940.

⁴ Further information on Bentley Priory: http://www.raf.mod.uk/rafbentleypriory/aboutus/bentleyprioryinwwii.cfm.

Chapter 20

¹ Winston Churchill, quoted in Churchill Museum and Cabinet War Rooms, http://cwr.iwm.org.uk/.

[2] Further information on Storey's Gate: http://cwr.iwm.org.uk/
server/show/ConWebDoc.923.

[3] Bitpipe.com, "Adaptive Enterprise," http://www.bitpipe.com/
tlist/Adaptive-Enterprise.html.

Chapter 21

[1] Source: Wikipedia.com.

Chapter 23

[1] Winston Churchill, quoted in Ian Speller, The Royal Navy
And Maritime Power in the Twentieth Century (New
York: Frank Cass, 2005).

[2] Ultra information was screened and passed indirectly to
Dowding by his superiors; he was not fully apprised of
the source until October 1940.

Chapter 24

[1] Richard Collier, "1940, August 16," Eagle Day—The Battle
of Britain, August 6–September 15, 1940, http://www.
humanitas-international.org/holocaust/1940tbse.htm.

[2] Winston Churchill, "The Few," August 20, 1940, The
Churchill Centre: Speeches & Quotes, http://
www.winstonchurchill.org/i4a/pages/index.
cfm?pageid=388#so_much_owed.

Chapter 25

[1] Dennis Richards, "The Fight at Odds," in Royal Air Force
1939–1945, Vol. 1 (London: HMSO, 1953),
http://ibiblio.org/hyperwar/UN/UK/UK-RAF-I/
index.html.

[2] Winston Churchill, quoted in "Finest Hour: September 1939–1941," 1940, The Churchill Centre: Churchill Facts, http://www.winstonchurchill.org/i4a/pages/index.cfm?pageid=220.

[3] Winston Churchill, "The Few," August 20, 1940, The Churchill Centre: Speeches & Quotes, http://www.winstonchurchill.org/i4a/pages/index.cfm?pageid=388#so_much_owed.

[4] Winston Churchill, quoted in "Finest Hour: September 1939–1941," 1940, The Churchill Centre: Churchill Facts, http://www.winstonchurchill.org/i4a/pages/index.cfm?pageid=220.

Chapter 26

[1] Dennis Richards, "The Fight at Odds," in *Royal Air Force 1939–1945*, Vol. 1 (London: HMSO, 1953), http://ibiblio.org/hyperwar/UN/UK/UK-RAF-I/index.html.

Chapter 27

[1] Winston Churchill, quoted in "Wit and Wisdom," 1940, The Churchill Centre: Publications & Resources, 2002–2002, http://www.winstonchurchill.org/i4a/pages/index.cfm?pageid=140.

[2] Winston Churchill, 1940, quoted in Quotations Page, http://www.quotationspage.com/quote/2087.html.

[3] Winston Churchill, 1940, quoted in Quotations Page, http://www.quotationspage.com/quote/2582.html.

[4] Encyclopedia Britannica Online, s.v. "Churchill, Winston," http://www.britannica.com/EBchecked/topic/117269/Sir-Winston-Churchill/60595/As-prime-minister.

[5] Voted Greatest Briton, ahead of Shakespeare, Darwin, Newton, Brunel, BBC poll 2003, http://news.bbc. co.uk/2/hi/entertainment/2509465.stm.

[6] Churchill is named *Time* magazine's man of the year for 1940, http://www.time.com/time personoftheyear/2006/walkup/, http://www. winstonchurchill.org/i4a/pages/index.cfm?pageid=360.

Appendix

[1] Martin Gilbert, *Continue to Pester, Nag and Bite: Churchill's War Leadership* (London: Pimlico, 2005).

[2] John Setear, "Sir Winston Churchill," University of Virginia School of Law: Why We Go to War (Topics), http:// faculty.virginia.edu/setear/courses/howweget/church. htm.

[3] Araminta Wordsworth, Financial Post, May 3, 2008.

[4] "Lord Beaverbrook," The Beaverbrook Foundation, http:// www.beaverbrookfoundation.org/lord-beaverbrook. php.

[5] RAF Bentley Priory, Royal Air Force, http://www.raf.mod.uk/rafbentleypriory/.

[6] "Timebase 1940," Timebase Multimedia Chronography™, http://www.humanitas-international.org/showcase/ chronography/timebase/1940tbse.htm.

Bibliography

Allen, Martin. 2003. *The Hitler/Hess deception: British intelligence's best-kept secret of the second world war.* New York: Harper Collins.

Battle of Britain Historical Society. http://www.battleofbritain1940.net/.

Briggs, Susan. 1975. *The home front: War years in Britain 1939–1945.* Boston: American Heritage.

British Tabulating Machine Company. http://www.jharper.demon.co.uk/btm1.htm.

Budiansky, Stephen. 2000. *Battle of wits: The complete story of codebreaking in World War II.* New York: Touchstone.

Cabinet War Rooms and Churchill Museum. http://cwr.iwm.org.uk/.

Churchill Centre: Bletchley Park Code Breaking. http://www.winstonchurchill.org/i4a/pages/index.cfm?pageid=407.

Churchill College: Churchill Archives Centre. http://www.chu.cam.ac.uk/archives/.

Deighton, Len. 1980. *Battle of Britain.* London: Jonathan Cape.

————. 1993. *Blood, tears, and folly: An objective look at World War II.* New York: HarperCollins.

————. 2000. *Fighter: The true story of the Battle of Britain.* London: Jonathan Cape.

German Enigma Cipher Machine—History of Solving. http://www.enigmahistory.org/enigma.html.

Highsmith, Jim. 2004. Agile project management: Creating innovative products. Boston: Pearson Education.

Imperial War Museum. http://www.iwm.org.uk.

Management Science—University of Strathclyde. http://www.strath.ac.uk/mansci/.

National Archives: NDAD: Statistical Departments. http://ndad.ulcc.ac.uk/datasets/AH/statistics.htm#gen.

PAN—Enigma German Secret Machine and the Remarkable Polish Success in Breaking the Code. http://pan.net/history/enigma/.

Project Management Institute. 2004. *A guide to the project Management body of knowledge.* 3rd ed. Newtown Square, PA: PMI Publications.

———. http://www.pmi.org/.

RAF Fighter Command Weekly Aircraft State July–November 1940. http://www.geocities.com/mchirnside/fcweek.htm.

RAF History. http://www.raf.mod.uk/history/.

RAF Sector Clocks. http://www.aeroclocks.com/Catalog_pages/sector.htm.

Real History and Churchill's War. http://www.fpp.co.uk/History/Churchill/WarRoom.html.

About the Author

 As the author behind the "Lessons from History" series, Mark Kozak-Holland brings years of experience as a consultant who helps Fortune-500 companies formulate projects that leverage emerging technologies. Since 1985 he has been straddling the business and IT worlds, making these projects happen. He is a certified business consultant, the author of several books, and a noted speaker. As a historian, Kozak-Holland seeks out the wisdom of the past to help others avoid repeating mistakes and to capture time-proven techniques. His lectures have been very popular at gatherings of project managers and CIOs.

Mark is very passionate about history and sees its potential use as an educational tool in business today. As a result, he has been developing the "Lessons from History" series for organisations, applying today's Information Technology (IT) to common business problems. It is written for primarily business and IT professionals looking for inspiration for their projects. It uses relevant historical case studies to examine how historical projects and emerging technologies of the past solved complex problems.

For thousands of years people have been running projects that leveraged emerging technologies of the time, to create unique and wonderful structures like the pyramids, buildings, or bridges. Similarly, people have gone on great expeditions and journeys and have raced their rivals in striving to be first, e.g., circumnavigating the world or conquering the poles. These were all forms of projects that required initiation, planning and design, production, implementation, and breakout.

The series looks at historical projects and then draws comparisons to challenges encountered in today's projects. It outlines the stages involved in delivering a complex project, providing a step-by-step guide to the project deliverables. It vividly describes the crucial lessons from historical projects and complements these with some of today's best practices.

This makes the whole learning experience more memorable. The series should inspire the reader, as these historical projects were achieved with a less sophisticated emerging technology.

Email: **mark.kozak-holl@sympatico.ca**

Web Site: **www.lessons-from-history.com**

LESSONS FROM
HISTORY

About the Series

This series is for primarily business and IT professionals looking for inspiration for their projects. Specifically, business managers responsible for solving business problems, or Project Managers (PMs) responsible for delivering business solutions through IT projects.

This series uses relevant historical case studies to examine how historical projects and emerging technologies of the past solved complex problems. It then draws comparisons to challenges encountered in today's IT projects.

This series benefits the reader in several ways:

- It outlines the stages involved in delivering a complex IT project providing a step-by-step guide to the project deliverables.

- It vividly describes the crucial lessons from historical projects and complements these with some of today's best practices.

- It makes the whole learning experience more memorable.

The series should inspire the reader as these historical projects were achieved with a lesser (inferior) technology.

Website: **http://www.lessons-from-history.com/**

Did you like this book?

If you enjoyed this book, you will find more
interesting books at

www.MMPubs.com

Please take the time to let us know how you liked
this book. Even short reviews of 2-3 sentences
can be helpful and may be used in our marketing
materials. If you take the time to post a review
for this book on Amazon.com, let us know when
the review is posted and you will receive a free
audiobook or ebook from our catalog. Simply
email the link to the review once it is live on
Amazon.com, with your name, and your mailing
address—send the email to orders@mmpubs.
com with the subject line "Book Review Posted on
Amazon."

If you have questions about this book, our
customer loyalty program, or our review rewards
program, please contact us at info@mmpubs.com.

Multi-Media Publications Inc.
Oshawa, Ontario, Canada

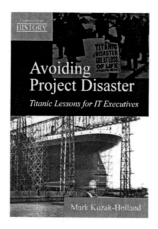

Avoiding Project Disaster: Titanic Lessons for IT Executives

Imagine you are in one of *Titanic's* lifeboats. As you look back at the wreckage site, you wonder what could have happened. What were the causes? How could things have gone so badly wrong?

Titanic's maiden voyage was a disaster waiting to happen as a result of the compromises made in the project that constructed the ship. This book explores how modern executives can take lessons from a nuts-and-bolts construction project like *Titanic* and use those lessons to ensure the right approach to developing online business solutions. Looking at this historical project as a model will prove to be incisive as it cuts away the layers of IT jargon and complexity.

Avoiding Project Disaster is about delivering IT projects in a world where being on time and on budget is not enough. You also need to be up and running around the clock for your customers and partners. This book will help you successfully maneuver through the ice floes of IT management in an industry with a notoriously high project failure rate.

ISBN: 1-895186-73-0   (paperback)

http://www.mmpubs.com/disaster

Titanic Lessons for IT Projects

Titanic Lessons for IT Projects analyzes the project that designed, built, and launched the ship, showing how compromises made during early project stages led to serious flaws in this supposedly "perfect ship." In addition, the book explains how major mistakes during the early days of the ship's operations led to the disaster. All of these disasterous compromises and mistakes were fully avoidable.

Entertaining and full of intriguing historical details, this companion book to *Avoiding Project Disaster: Titanic Lessons for IT Executives* helps project managers and IT executives see the impact of decisions similar to the ones that they make every day. An easy read full of illustrations and photos to help explain the story and to help drive home some simple lessons.

ISBN: 1-895186-26-9   (paperback)

http://www.mmpubs.com/titanic

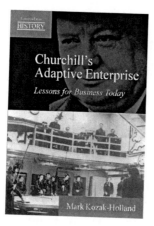

Churchill's Adaptive Enterprise: Lessons for Business Today

This book analyzes a period of time from World War II when Winston Churchill, one of history's most famous leaders, faced near defeat for the British in the face of sustained German attacks. The book describes the strategies he used to overcome incredible odds and turn the tide on the impending invasion. The historical analysis is done through a modern business and information technology lens, describing Churchill's actions and strategy using modern business tools and techniques. Aimed at business executives, IT managers, and project managers, the book extracts learnings from Churchill's experiences that can be applied to business problems today. Particular themes in the book are knowledge management, information portals, adaptive enterprises, and organizational agility.

ISBN: 1-895186-19-6 (paperback)

http://www.mmpubs.com/churchill

Project Lessons from The Great Escape (Stalag Luft III)

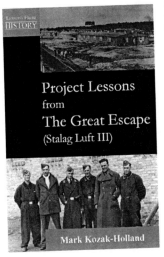

While you might think your project plan is perfect, would you bet your life on it? In World War II, a group of 220 captured airmen did just that—they staked the lives of everyone in the camp on the success of a project to secretly build a series of tunnels out of a prison camp their captors thought was escape proof. The prisoners formally structured their work as a project, using the project organization techniques of the day. This book analyzes their efforts using modern project management methods and the nine knowledge areas of the *Guide to the Project Management Body of Knowledge* (*PMBoK Guide*). Learn from the successes and mistakes of a project where people really put their lives on the line.

ISBN: 9781895186802 (paperback)

http://www.mmpubs.com/escape

Printed in the United States
152948LV00002B/4/P